Holding Companies and Their Published Accounts

Limitations of a Balance Sheet

Sir Gilbert Garnsey

Garland Publishing, Inc.
New York & London   1982

These facsimiles have been made from copies in the library of the American Institute of Certified Public Accountants. Reprinted by permission of Gee & Co. (Publishers), Ltd.

Library of Congress Cataloging in Publication Data

Garnsey, Gilbert Francis, Sir, 1883–1932.
　Holding companies and their published accounts ; Limitations of a balance sheet.

　　(Accountancy in transition)
　　Reprint (1st work). Originally published: London : Gee, 1923.
　　Reprint (2nd work). Originally published in: Proceedings of the autumnal meeting / Institute of Chartered Accountants in England and Wales. London : Gee, 1928.
　　1. Holding companies—Accounting.　2. Holding companies—Great Britain—Accounting.　I. Garnsey, Gilbert Francis, Sir, 1883-1932. Limitations of a balance sheet. 1982.　II. Title.　III. Series.
HF5686.H6G37　　1982　　　657'.96　　　82-48364
ISBN 0-8240-5315-X

The volumes in this series are printed on acid-free, 250-year-life paper.

Printed in the United States of America

HOLDING COMPANIES

AND THEIR

PUBLISHED ACCOUNTS

BY

SIR GILBERT GARNSEY, K.B.E., F.C.A.

———

LONDON:
GEE & CO. (PUBLISHERS) LTD., 6 KIRBY STREET, E.C.1.
—
1923.

Preface

THIS book is, for practical purposes, a reprint of a paper read by me before the London Members of the Institute of Chartered Accountants on the 12th December 1922. Some 1,000 copies of this paper were printed at the time and distributed privately to members of the Institute and friends. At the request of a number of my professional and other friends who are interested in the subject, it has been decided to print the paper in book form.

The text is substantially the same as in the original paper, but some slight additions have been made in order to make its meaning clearer, while Appendix II is entirely new. In that Appendix will be found a number of examples of Published Balance Sheets as furnished to shareholders, and they are printed here (without any comment) by the kind permission of the respective companies, so that readers may see for themselves some forms adopted in practice.

It is hoped that this treatise may be of some service to all interested and especially to practising members of the profession. The subject matter is a comparatively new one in this country and is likely to be of increasing importance in the future.

I shall be grateful for any suggestions which will render the book more useful to its readers.

GILBERT GARNSEY.

3 FREDERICK'S PLACE,
LONDON, E.C.2.

September 1923.

Contents

CHAPTER.		PAGE
I.	Introductory	1
II.	Advantages and Disadvantages of Amalgamations	3
III.	Amalgamations through a Holding Company	5
IV.	Trading and Non-Trading Companies	11
V.	Methods of Presentation of Accounts..	13
VI.	Method I.—The " Legal " Balance Sheet	17
VII.	Method II.—The " Legal " Balance Sheet, together with Balance Sheets of Subsidiaries	47
VIII.	Method III.—The " Legal " Balance Sheet, together with a Summary of Assets and Liabilities of Subsidiaries	52
IX.	Method IV.—Amalgamated or Consolidated Balance Sheets	57
X.	Some Notes on Taxation as affecting Holding Companies :—	
	Income Tax	76
	Excess Profits Duty	78
	Corporation Profits Tax ..	81

Appendix I.

Illustrations.

Holding Company's Balance Sheet :—	
Preliminary Draft	86
Amended Draft	88
Subsidiary Companies :—	
A Preliminary Draft	90
B Do.	92
C Do.	94
D Do.	94
Preliminary Summary Statement of Assets and Liabilities of Subsidiary Companies only	96
Detailed Consolidated Balance Sheet of Holding Company and Subsidiary Companies ..	100

Appendix II.

Examples of Actual Published Balance Sheets.

British Companies	111-183
American Companies	185-208

Chapter I

INTRODUCTORY.

The expression "Holding Company" is one which was little known in this country until recent years, and is intended to describe the company whose function is to hold the shares or stock of one or more concerns with the intention of controlling their operations. Holding Companies have no specific legal recognition as such, and are governed by the regulations of the Companies Acts in exactly the same way as other limited liability concerns.

It may be thought that the ordinary trust or investment company should be called a Holding Company because its purpose is to own the shares or stock of other concerns and to receive the dividends thereon. The term, however, is not applied to this class of company which, as a rule, has only a comparatively small holding in the capital of the undertakings in which it is interested, and does not control the operations of any of them.

It is not uncommon for companies to be formed for the specific purpose of holding investments in trust as the nominees of another company, so as to save the trouble and expense involved in transfers on the death of an individual nominee. They are often referred to as Holding Companies, though the term as understood amongst accountants is hardly applicable.

The class of company with which it is proposed to deal is the one which acquires the whole or a controlling interest in the share capital (generally ordinary shares, though not necessarily limited to these) of one or more distinct businesses, and thereby for practical purposes effectively amalgamating them and consolidating their interests, while at the same time each of the separate undertakings continues its own sphere of operations and retains its existence as a separate entity. These separate concerns are generally referred to as subsidiary or constituent undertakings, while the company owning their share capital and controlling their operations is called the Holding or Parent Company.

It is perhaps desirable at this point to state that while certain views may be expressed in this book they are put forward having regard to the facts and circumstances set out, and it should be understood that the writer feels himself open to adopt a different point of view where the facts are not identical or where the circumstances appear to warrant a different treatment. It is important to state this, as accountants are often confronted with statements made or views expressed and asked to reconcile them, perhaps, with other views expressed on a particular case under review and under entirely different circumstances. It is not usually very difficult, but technical explanations are not always thoroughly understood outside the profession.

Chapter II

ADVANTAGES AND DISADVANTAGES OF AMALGAMATIONS.

Consolidation is of wide and increasing interest to modern business men, and especially to accountants. It has increased rapidly during the last decade, as the advantages to be derived therefrom have become more widely known. The realisation that, by combination of interests rather than by competition, activities could be more fully and economically developed and bigger things achieved; while the necessity for not disturbing the organisation of existing companies and the need for preserving the names and goodwill of businesses of reputation, led to the idea that the benefits of combination could be obtained without disturbing existing organisations by the parties to the proposed combine forming a new company and taking shares therein to represent the value of their respective businesses. The necessity of becoming independent of outside sources of supply of raw materials has resulted in many combinations, and this was specially noticeable throughout the late war.

There is now hardly any class of commercial activity in this country in which the influence of consolidation is not felt.

Among the many advantages to be derived therefrom may be mentioned elimination of ruinous competition, control of prices (which does not necessarily mean exorbitant enhancement), pooling of technical experience, economy in production, distribution of production economically, efficiency in management by means of wider field for comparison by results, control of sources of raw material supplies, concentration of classes of product to obtain maximum output at minimum prices, reduction of overhead expenses, avoidance of duplication in management, stocks, selling expenses, &c.

On the other hand it has its dangers, such as the possibility of monopoly, fraudulent promotion and management, complexity of company organisation, and, consequently, a tendency to obscure results and thus deceive shareholders as to the real value of their holdings.

This applies particularly to concerns which are controlled by means of a Holding Company and where there are shareholders whose shares have not been acquired whether preference or ordinary. It is obvious that in cases of this character, while transactions carried through by any one or more of the subsidiary undertakings may be to the advantage of the consolidation as a whole, yet at the same time they may seriously affect the interests of the outside shareholders. In this connection such transactions as inter-company buying and selling should be fair to all, and not merely be in the interests of the Holding Company or the group as a whole. Similarly, a loan from one subsidiary company to another without security may be perfectly reasonable looking at the concerns as a whole, and yet may be quite unfair if there are outside shareholders.

There is also the danger of oppressive treatment of minority shareholders where, for instance, a subsidiary company pays no dividends but the parent company takes credit for its share of the profits and obtains the funds by means of advances from the subsidiary. While it is true that undistributed profits of a subsidiary should not be declared as dividend by the Holding Company yet for practical purposes the latter gets the full benefit of ownership without distributing any dividends to minority shareholders of the subsidiary.

Chapter III

AMALGAMATIONS THROUGH A HOLDING COMPANY.

It is not the intention to enter into a discussion of the bases upon which a Holding Company may acquire its interest in subsidiary undertakings or to deal in any way with the principles governing the amalgamation of businesses by means of a Holding Company. This book is more concerned with the presentation of the figures to the shareholders after the subsidiary undertakings have been acquired and the merger becomes an accomplished fact. At the same time a few general remarks will not be out of place and may assist in dealing with some of the points which arise on the accounts.

Businesses desiring to amalgamate (as distinct from a mere pooling of profits) generally do so in one of two ways. The first—the direct merger—where an existing company, or one formed for the purpose, takes over the actual assets and liabilities of the other undertakings and amalgamates them with its own, the other concerns being wound up and ceasing to exist. The second—the indirect merger through a Holding Company where a company formed for the purpose, or one already in existence, acquires the shares of the other concerns and not their actual assets and liabilities.

The Holding Company method of amalgamation or consolidation of interests has become very widespread in recent years, and it is the most effective way in which an amalgamation can be brought about when it is desired to interfere as little as possible with the existing organisations.

The process is simple and less costly than the direct merger method, which involves the taking over of the assets and the liquidation of the other concerns.

Further, the Holding Company merger does not necessarily involve the interference with the debenture-holders, the preference shareholders or a minority of ordinary shareholders who are unwilling to dispose of their holdings. In fact, it is only necessary to acquire the ordinary shares or a majority of those shares which have the voting power and thereby control the company. This is extremely important where the subsidiary undertakings have obtained money on debentures, preference shares, or on similar securities at low rates of interest.

In the direct form of amalgamation, involving the liquidation of the old concerns, it would be necessary to repay at par the debentures and also the preference shareholders unless they could be induced to convert their holdings into some securities of the new company. In the latter event they would no doubt require a higher rate of interest or some similar concession. In such circumstances, if the market value of the debentures and preference shares is less than par or the value of the exchanged securities, obviously there is a direct loss. Similarly, there is the ordinary shareholder who does not assent to the scheme, he would have to be paid out probably also at a loss. These losses fall automatically upon the other ordinary shareholders, because the value of the business as a whole being the same whatever the method of amalgamation, the more that is given to the debenture-holders or the preference or non-assenting ordinary shareholders, the less remains for the other ordinary shareholders.

The losses would not fall upon the other ordinary shareholders if the existing undertaking is continued and not wound up, for the reason that the debentures, preference shares and non-assenting ordinary shares are not disturbed. To put it in another way it is only necessary to value the ordinary shares if these have the control, and with debentures and preference shares already in existence at low rates of interest, this means a higher return for the ordinary shareholder and consequently a higher value for the shares. If the debentures and preference shares are to be paid off, there will be a lower return on the ordinary shares and consequently the value is correspondingly reduced.

Formation of Holding Companies.

As a rule the procedure is to form a new company (though this is not essential) to acquire from the shareholders the shares they hold in the undertakings about to be amalgamated either for cash or what is more likely, in exchange for shares in the Holding Company, the terms and basis of exchange in any case having been agreed beforehand. The result is that the profits of the various undertakings whose shares have been thus acquired find their way to the Holding Company, which, in turn, distributes them amongst its shareholders. It follows that a shareholder in one of the old undertakings who has taken shares in the Holding Company in exchange for his shares, instead of being dependent upon the profits and assets of the old undertaking alone, becomes interested in the profits and assets of all the concerns whose shares have been purchased by the Holding Company. The shareholder looks to the Holding Company for his profits and the security for his capital while the Holding Company, in turn, looks to the undertakings whose shares it has acquired.

It sometimes happens that instead of forming a new company, an existing undertaking, perhaps the largest of the companies contemplating the merging of their interests, acquires the necessary shares of the remaining concerns to obtain control, and in this way an amalgamation is brought about through the larger concern, which then becomes the Holding Company.

Cases also are known where a large undertaking, with a view to facilitating the carrying on of its business or for other reasons, forms one or more subsidiary companies to take over the assets and liabilities of certain sections or departments of the business, or even the whole business, taking as consideration for the net assets the shares of the subsidiary undertakings. In this way also Holding Companies are created.

An important question arises as to what shares in the subsidiary undertakings it is necessary to acquire to obtain control, and this naturally is a matter to be decided according to the circumstances of each individual case. As a rule, at all events in this country, the acquisition of the ordinary shares, or a majority of them, would probably be sufficient to constitute effective control. This may be sufficient for the purpose in view of those who are carrying out the amalgamation, though a three-fourths majority would be necessary to carry a special resolution, for example, to alter the articles of association.

Position of Preference Shareholders with Special Rights.

Preference shareholders, who usually have voting rights only when their interest is in arrear or their capital in jeopardy, are sometimes entitled under the regulations of a company to attend and vote at all meetings, and, moreover, are in some cases entitled to share in the surplus assets with the ordinary shareholders. Where such is the case it may become necessary to acquire certain of the preference shares before effective control of the undertaking is obtained or to enter into an agreement to guarantee their dividends. It is probable, however, that this will not often happen, but should it be necessary the difficulties of the amalgamation will be increased, especially, as so often happens, if the preference shares are widely held. Separate meetings of the preference shareholders may be necessary unless the shares required can be obtained in the market or privately. In any event the requisite consents of the shareholders affected must be obtained and the larger the number the more difficult it may become.

Boards of Directors and Control.

When these preliminaries have been attended to, and the amalgamation has been effected, the work of re-organisation and co-ordination begins. The control being exercised through the Holding Company, some re-arrangement of the boards of directors of the various undertakings is usually necessary. The board of the Holding Company generally consists of one or more of the directors from each of the subsidiary companies, and this board directs the policy and controls the operations of the consolidation as a whole, while the boards of directors of the subsidiary undertakings are appointed by them and act as their nominees. The subsidiary companies are thereby, in effect, managed in exactly the same way as if they were integral parts or branches of the organisation of the Holding Company and yet retain the legal fiction of separate companies. It is also possible that one or more of the directors from each of the subsidiary undertakings will join the board of the other subsidiary companies or may retire altogether, while a committee of directors will often manage the affairs of the whole organisation. The re-arrangement does not always take place in this way, and the peculiarities of the situation arising from each case have to be considered and effect given to them.

Cases are not unknown where, although the Holding Company owns a large majority of the ordinary shares, it has been found inadvisable, on grounds of policy or from personal or other causes, difficult to deal with, to exercise any real control at all over the affairs of a subsidiary undertaking which may thus carry on its business exactly as it has always done and without any regard to the real interests of the merger. This state of affairs does not as a rule last for long, and the time soon comes when the paramount interests of the consolidation make it incumbent to deal with the situation and to bring the affairs of this concern within the ambit of the organisation as a whole.

Chapter IV

TRADING AND NON-TRADING COMPANIES.

There are, broadly, two classes of Holding Companies, the trading companies—those which, in addition to holding the controlling interest in and directing the affairs of other companies, themselves carry on a trade or business. The second class is the non-trading companies—which by their regulations have no power to carry on a trade or business other than the holding of investments, and whose sole functions are to hold the shares, to direct the operations, and to receive and re-distribute the dividends declared by the subsidiary companies.

A Holding Company which also carries on trading would naturally have in its Balance Sheet, in addition to the shares in the subsidiary undertakings, assets of the character usually held by trading concerns, such as buildings, plant, stocks, debtors, cash and so forth, while in the case of the non-trading Holding Company, practically the only asset would be the Holding Company's interest in subsidiary concerns in the form of investments in shares and any advances on loan or current account.

The distinction between trading and non-trading Holding Companies may be important from the point of view of the legal position in regard to the writing down by the Holding Company of the cost of its investments in subsidiary undertakings before the payment of dividends, assuming the shares had diminished in value since they were acquired.

In the case of the non-trading concern it would seem that the Holding Company could not legally be called upon to write down the cost, inasmuch as the investments would be regarded as capital assets (or fixed capital), and the decision in *Verner v. General Commercial Trust* would apparently hold good.

With the trading concern, however, the legal position is not so clear, and, so far as the writer is aware, has not been definitely decided by the Courts.

At the same time it is desirable to point out that the above case might not be held to apply to a Holding Company which has investments in manufacturing and trading companies sufficient to enable it to *control and carry on their business,* as distinct from an investment entitling the owner merely to receive the dividends declared as was the case in the *General Commercial Trust.* In such cases it might perhaps be held that the Holding Company must provide for losses on trading incurred by the subsidiaries on the ground that solely from an income, as distinct from a capital, point of view the investment has depreciated to that extent.

In any event the remarks which follow deal with the position of both classes of companies from an accountant's point of view and without any regard whatever to the possible legal position in any particular case which would require detailed consideration and possibly special treatment.

Chapter V

METHODS OF PRESENTING ACCOUNTS.

There are, roughly speaking, four methods of presenting the accounts of Holding Companies, and it is proposed to consider the advantages and disadvantages of each method, the result obtained, and to examine in detail many of the important points which arise in connection with the accounts presented in each of the four ways.

The four methods are :—

(i) To publish only the Holding Company's Balance Sheet and Profit and Loss Account, treating the interest in subsidiary companies as an Investment in the Balance Sheet and including in the profits the dividends actually received from the subsidiary undertakings.

The total profits and/or losses of the subsidiary undertakings are sometimes taken up in the Holding Company's Balance Sheet and Profit and Loss Account irrespective of what dividends are actually declared and paid.

(ii) To publish the Balance Sheet and Profit and Loss Account of the Holding Company as in (i) and to present simultaneously the separate Balance Sheets and Profit and Loss Accounts of all the subsidiary companies.

(iii) To publish the Balance Sheet and Profit and Loss Account of the Holding Company as in (i) and also at the same time as a separate statement a Summary of the Assets and Liabilities of all the subsidiary undertakings taken together.

(iv) To publish either separately or along with the Holding Company's Balance Sheet (as in (i)) a consolidated Balance Sheet of the whole undertaking amalgamating the assets and liabilities of all the subsidiaries with those of the Holding Company and a consolidated Profit and Loss Account embracing the profits and losses of all the companies.

If the Holding Company does not own the whole of the capital of the subsidiary companies the separate statement and consolidated Balance Sheet referred to in (iii) and (iv) above should show as a liability the total interests of all outside shareholders. This may include the whole or a number of the preference shares and also a minority interest in the ordinary share capital.

A variation is sometimes suggested in the treatment of minority interests of subsidiary companies and, instead of showing it as a liability as indicated above, only the proportion of each asset and liability of the subsidiary companies attributable to the capital held by the Holding Company are set out. This procedure is not to be recommended, and gives rise to some peculiar results as will be seen later.

Examples in Appendix I.

It is now proposed to consider in detail each method of presenting the accounts, and in order to enable this to be followed the more readily an example is given in Appendix I of a Balance Sheet of a Holding Company and four subsidiary companies, referred to as A., B., C., and D.

It will be noted that these accounts are all described as Preliminary Draft Balance Sheets, for the reason that they are not drawn up in the form

PRESENTATION OF ACCOUNTS

in which they would necessarily be published, but have been drafted deliberately, giving sufficient details to illustrate some of the points to which reference will hereafter be made.

For the present purpose it is assumed that the four subsidiary companies are all managed and controlled by the Board of the Holding Company or by their nominees cn the boards of the four undertakings.

The Balance Sheet of the Holding Company shows that it owns one-half the total preference share issue and nine-tenths of the ordinary shares of subsidiary company A., as well as 17,400 out of 17,500 shares of subsidiary company B., and 51 per cent. of the shares of subsidiary company D. Some of these have been acquired at a premium and some at a discount.

On the other hand, subsidiary company B. owns the whole of the ordinary shares of subsidiary company C., while it also shows as an asset a considerable number of shares in the Holding Company.

It will be seen that the Holding Company has made considerable advances to subsidiary A., which appear under the heads of "Sundry Debtors" and "Bills Receivable." On the other side of this Balance Sheet attention is drawn to the reserve, which includes a sum of £120,000 for premium on the issue of ordinary shares of the Holding Company, in payment of the ordinary shares acquired in subsidiary A., while the Profit and Loss Account shows that its net profit includes a very considerable dividend from subsidiary B., but no dividend whatever from subsidiaries A. or D. The Holding Company has, however, made a large profit on the sale of goods purchased from subsidiary A., and taken credit for interest charged against that company on advances, while its own trading shows a loss of £100,000. Taken as a whole, there is a substantial profit shown, and the Balance

Sheet appears to reveal a flourishing state of affairs.

A glance at the Balance Sheet of subsidiary A. shows that this company has made heavy losses and has had to borrow substantial sums from the Holding Company and subsidiary B., besides having large outstanding creditors. The greater portion of its stocks on hand have been acquired from subsidiary B. at a substantial profit to the latter. Generally the Balance Sheet of subsidiary A. shows a bad position.

With regard to subsidiary B., it is obvious on looking at the figures that this is the company which is responsible for the large profits, practically the whole of which have been paid away in dividends to the Holding Company. It will be noticed that since the date of the purchase of this company's shares by the Holding Company, a considerable dividend has been paid out of the surplus existing at that time. The shares held by this company in subsidiary C. and in the Holding Company have been acquired at a premium, while it also has advances to subsidiary A.

The special point in connection with subsidiary C. is that the preference shareholders are entitled to share with the ordinary shareholders in the surplus on a winding-up.

Subsidiary D. does not call for any special comment at this stage.

An amended draft Balance Sheet of the Holding Company which more correctly sets out the real position is given and will be referred to later.

A preliminary summary statement of the surplus assets of the four subsidiary companies A., B., C., and D. is also given, as well as a detailed consolidated Balance Sheet of the Holding Company and the four subsidiary undertakings showing the workings in full, so that anyone who desires to see how the figures have been put together may be able to do so readily.

Chapter VI

METHOD (i).—THE "LEGAL" BALANCE SHEET.

To publish only the Holding Company's Balance Sheet and Profit and Loss Account, showing the interest in subsidiary companies as an Investment.

Advantages and Disadvantages.

In this country it is more usual to publish the Holding Company Balance Sheet in this form, which sets out only the actual assets and liabilities of the Holding Company and does not complicate the statement by the introduction of assets and liabilities of other companies, which, although controlled by it, are nevertheless carrying on business as separate legal entities.

From the creditors' point of view a Balance Sheet prepared in this way is essential to enable them to form an opinion of the financial condition of the company against which they would have to proceed if occasion arose.

Again, if the Holding Company wanted to raise money on debentures or shares with a charge upon its own assets, it would find it necessary to prepare a Balance Sheet showing its own assets and liabilities alone before an accurate opinion of the security offered could be formed, although it might be supplemented by a statement of the net surplus assets of the associated undertakings.

It will, moreover, be claimed that this Balance Sheet is the more legal one based upon the legal status of the Holding Company as a separate and distinct corporation and one which would be required to be furnished to the authorities at Somerset House for filing purposes under the Companies Acts. It is not, however, thought that the authorities could or would refuse to accept Balance Sheets prepared in the consolidated form referred to later and within the writer's experience they have been accepted.

One of the advantages attaching to the Holding Company's Balance Sheet in the separate or legal form is that it is all that is legally necessary for the directors to publish.

Some might say that this is a distinct disadvantage, because directors should be induced to disclose to shareholders as much information as possible not only in connection with the concern in which they are directly interested but also of the subsidiary companies in which their interest is just as great although it may be indirect. While there is a lot of truth in this it is also true to say that the legal Balance Sheet enables the directors to prevent the disclosure of vital information to competitors regarding their interest in subsidiary undertakings. Further it admits of the equalisation of the income of the parent company from one period to another by the retention of undistributed profits in the accounts of the subsidiaries.

There is no doubt that the question of disclosure to competitors is of considerable importance and is often the deciding factor against any change in the form of the published accounts. Shareholders as a rule are quick to appreciate the dangers attending a too full statement of the affairs of their company and rely to an almost unlimited extent upon the advice tendered to them by their board.

On the other hand, cases are not unknown where directors, looking for an excuse, seize upon this to furnish their shareholders with as little information as possible. Shareholders, however, are now

METHOD I.—PRESENTATION

beginning to understand and to ask for more details, and experience has shown that it is all to the good to give it to them if it can be done without injury to the company's vital interest.

At a recent meeting of a well-known limited company the chairman, referring to the Balance Sheet, said:—

> "It is frequently stated as a matter of complaint that the Balance Sheet of a company like ours does not tell the full story about the position of the business, and that shareholders are quite in the dark as to what is really behind such an item as 'Cost of Shares in Constituent Companies, £17,334,564.' It is said that parent or holding companies are able to screen the true position of affairs and that such a document as this gives no indication as to whether the business of the operative companies is prosperous or the reverse. I need hardly point out to you that, although we may, in fact, own practically the whole of these businesses, so long as they remain separate legal entities as distinct companies we are not entitled to put into our Balance Sheet the land, buildings, &c., they own, but can, perforce, only indicate the shares we hold at what was given for them in our own share capital and cash. But, while this form of legal Balance Sheet is thus narrowly prescribed for us, and we have no option in the matter, we have every desire that shareholders should have the fullest possible information as to the real position and know what actually constitutes their assets."

It is doubtful whether the legal Balance Sheet, as usually seen nowadays unaccompanied by any further particulars concerning the general position of the allied undertakings, really gives the shareholders the information to which they are entitled. It fails to recognise the practical nature of the relationship existing between the Holding Company and its subsidiaries. The treatment may be justified on legal and technical grounds in that the Holding Company merely owns the shares, but it is a method which is open to criticism from the point of view of an investor and lends itself to abuse in the hands of an unscrupulous management. Moreover, from the business standpoint, the parent company virtually owns and actually controls the surplus assets of its subsidiaries which the shares represent.

With some companies it can certainly be said that the legal Balance Sheet does not show the true position of the Holding Company, and gives little or no information of the consolidation as a whole.

It is submitted that in every such case where it is clear that the Holding Company's Balance Sheet does not of itself give a full and fair statement of the position, as, for example, where a considerable portion of the capital is invested in subsidiary concerns, then it should be supplemented either by an aggregated statement of the assets and liabilities of all the undertakings, including the Holding Company, or by a statement of the total assets and liabilities of all the subsidiary enterprises whichever may seem the more appropriate for the occasion.

Without some such statement it would be possible to conceal the real state of affairs of the subsidiary companies, what profits or losses they were making, what their assets consist of, what liabilities have been incurred, and so on, as these facts would not appear in the Holding Company's accounts at all.

In the case of the concern referred to above, the chairman proceeded to inform the shareholders that a consolidated statement of assets and liabilities of the parent company and its subsidiaries had been prepared, and he gave them the figures by way of supplementary information. This is worthy of special mention as one of the few cases of its kind in this country—a precedent which it is hoped will be followed by all similar concerns in the future.

Shareholdings—How set out in Balance Sheet.

The amount representing the shares held in subsidiary or constituent undertakings is often included in the Balance Sheet in the general head of Investments along with other investments of a totally different character without being so disclosed, and loans or balances on current account owing by or to subsidiary undertakings occasionally appear under the general heading of Sundry Debtors or Sundry Creditors as if they were not of a special character. It is clear that each case must be decided according to the facts surrounding it, and a definite principle cannot be laid down that will apply to every case, but as a rule the item Shares or Holdings in Subsidiary or Allied Companies should not appear under the general heading of Investments in the parent company's Balance Sheet. The example in Appendix I illustrates this point. It would clearly be wrong in the Balance Sheet of the Holding Company to include the shares in the subsidiary undertakings under the head of Investments in the same category as War Stocks. They are of a totally different character.

The items included under this head are, as a rule, investments of a readily realisable character which have probably been acquired by way of temporary investment of cash funds. They are shown in the Balance Sheet as current assets near the item Cash, as indicating that they are of a liquid character and may be relied upon to supply funds in case of emergency.

This hardly applies to shares in controlled subsidiary companies which are not usually held for the purposes of re-sale at all, but are intended to be held and used for the purpose of earning profit. In other words they should be regarded in the light of capital or fixed assets and so treated in the

Balance Sheet of the Holding Company under a separate heading such as "Shares (or Holdings) in Subsidiary Companies."

It is possible that the share capital of the constituent undertakings may not be represented by tangible assets at all and may have been entirely lost in trading, as, for example, in the case of subsidiary A. in Appendix I.

Moreover, the shares, failing a ready market which rarely exists, are of an indirect character in the sense that in the liquidation of a subsidiary concern the parent company, in respect of its shares, would (subject to minority interests) receive only the balance of the assets remaining after all liabilities and prior charges had been paid. In other words, the investments represent the Holding Company's right to the subsidiary's net surplus assets.

The heading Trade Investments does not wholly meet the case, unless it is clearly explained that the item consists of investments in undertakings which are controlled and unless it is so set out in the Balance Sheet as to make it clear that it is not in the nature of a current asset.

Naturally, if the assets of the subsidiaries were all of a current nature, such as stock, debts, cash, &c., which could be made use of by the parent company, a different position might arise, but this is seldom found to be the case.

At the same time it is realised that instances may be cited where some justification could be shown for including the item under some heading other than the separate one suggested above.

As to whether the names of the subsidiaries and the numbers and denominations of the various shares held should be set out in full on the face of the Balance Sheet depends upon the circumstances. Wherever possible it should be done, but it could hardly be considered essential to do so and might not always be advisable from the point of view of competitors.

Amounts due from Subsidiary Companies.

Another important matter is the treatment of loans or advances or debit balances on current or other account with subsidiary undertakings. Cases will no doubt occur to everyone where the true state of affairs would not be shown if these balances were allowed to remain in the Parent Company's Balance Sheet under the general head of Sundry Debtors. By increasing the current assets in this way the Balance Sheet might show a better position than is justified and thereby it might improperly facilitate borrowing by the Parent Company. As a rule these advances to subsidiaries are not current assets, although the manner in which they are shown might give this impression.

Subsidiary companies which are extending their business are often financed by means of loans from the Holding Company rather than by the raising of additional capital. The subsidiary undertaking may find it necessary to borrow from the Parent Company to meet capital expenditure which is not realisable at all as a going concern, or for the purpose of purchasing larger stocks or to meet trading losses or to repay capital liabilities such as debentures.

It becomes necessary, therefore, in considering the debit balance against a subsidiary to ascertain what is represented by it in the subsidiary undertaking. It may be by capital expenditure or trading losses; in fact, the greater the losses the more is money likely to be required. In many cases the loans or other debit balances are as much a part of the capital of the subsidiary company as that represented by the shares in the hands of the Parent Company, and where this is so, they should be so treated in the Holding Company's Balance Sheet.

If the constituent company is not in a position immediately to repay the amounts owing or is not likely to do so they should not appear among sundry debtors of the Holding Company or under current assets at all. It is not enough to say that the subsidiary undertaking is in a position to borrow money on debenture or otherwise and to repay the Holding Company if it has not, in fact, done so.

There may be cases where it would be a more accurate statement to divide the debit balance and to include such portion of it as has been paid or is likely to be paid in cash (as, for example, final dividends of a subsidiary company) with other debts due to the Holding Company under Sundry Debtors.

Here, again, each case must be decided upon its merits, but where it is considered that it would be wrong to include the item in Sundry Debtors it is better that it should be shown with the item representing the investment in shares supplementing the wording accordingly or set out separately under some such appropriate heading as "Advances to Subsidiary Companies," adding the amount to the item representing the shares and carrying to the total column the sum of the two. If it is so desired a note could be put under the two items showing how much is represented by fixed and current assets respectively in the subsidiary undertakings.

In the example in Appendix I it will be seen that the loan by the Holding Company to subsidiary A. is represented by losses or by fixed assets and is certainly not of a current nature. If subsidiary A. were to fail, the Holding Company might take its share with the other creditors of the amount realised in the liquidation after payment of the

METHOD I.—PRESENTATION

debenture stock, but it might not be in the interest of the Holding Company or of the consolidation as a whole that this subsidiary undertaking should go into liquidation, and that this is so here appears to be illustrated by the item "Stocks" in the Balance Sheet, which would seem to indicate that subsidiary A. is an important outlet for the goods of subsidiary B. This means in effect that the Holding Company would have to make itself responsible for the payment of the other creditors of subsidiary A., and so far from receiving money would largely increase the amount of its advances.

Amounts due to Subsidiary Companies.

With regard to balances due *to* subsidiary companies these should be set out as liabilities in the Balance Sheet as a separate item and not included under the general head of Sundry Creditors. Amounts due to one subsidiary company may be set off against advances made to the same concern, but should not be deducted from advances to other subsidiaries. While they may be related transactions they are distinct in the sense that on a winding-up there is no set off and the liabilities would have to be paid to the one company and the advances collected from the other concerns.

" Cost " where Consideration is Exchange of Shares at a Premium.

So much for the setting out of the items on the face of the Balance Sheet. It is now necessary to consider the amount at which the investments might appear therein, whether at cost or at what value.

In the books of the Parent Company the shares it holds in subsidiary or constituent undertakings will no doubt appear at cost, i.e. the amount paid in cash or in its own shares issued in exchange. In the case of an exchange of shares the transaction will probably have taken into account the value of the Holding Company's shares at the time the transaction was entered into (it may be there is an official market quotation), and if this value should be in excess of the par value, the Holding Company might regard the excess as a premium upon the issue of its own shares. An example of this is given in Appendix I, where it will be seen that the Holding Company acquired the ordinary shares of subsidiary A. for £150,000, satisfied by the issue of 30,000 of its own shares which presumably stood in the market at the time, or were considered to be of the value of £5 each, or at a premium of £4 per share. The Holding Company has taken the premium of £120,000 to its Reserve Account. The Balance Sheet of subsidiary A. shows that it would not be correct to treat it in this way as the reserve does not exist. As to whether it existed at the date the shares were acquired, having regard to the price paid for them, would depend upon the real financial position at that time which is not clear and would require investigation. From the information now available, however, it is suggested that the cost to the Holding Company should be stated at £30,000, viz.: the par value of the shares issued. In other words, the premium should be deducted from the "cost" and not shown as a Reserve.

It may be asked, is this always correct? The answer must obviously depend entirely upon the circumstances of each case. Speaking generally, however, the premium should be deducted from the cost in every case where it is not represented in the subsidiary company by a surplus of tangible assets (other than goodwill) over liabilities, including shares not acquired, and after deducting from the surplus the par value of the shares of the Holding Company issued in exchange. Assume, as an example, a company having a capital of £100, reserve £100, and net tangible assets, after deducting liabilities of £200, and that the Holding Company acquired the whole of the share capital (i.e.

£100) by the issue of 50 of its own £1 shares, which then stood in the market at, say, £4 each or at a premium of £3. There is a surplus of assets over liabilities of the company acquired of £200, and there seems no reason why in such a case the premium of £3 (viz., £150) should not appear amongst the Holding Company's reserves though not as part of the General Reserve Fund unless it is ear-marked definitely as a premium.

If, in the above example, the surplus tangible assets were £100 and £100 represented goodwill, it is submitted that the Holding Company would only be justified in showing £50 of the premium as a reserve and the balance of £100 should be deducted from the cost of the shares, showing a net cost of £100 in its own books.

Whether the premium would be available for revenue purposes depends upon the company's memorandum and articles of association.

It may be said that if this premium is allowed to be shown as a reserve in the Holding Company's Balance Sheet, then in the whole merger it will appear twice, in that it may also appear in the constituent company's Balance Sheet. This is undoubtedly so, but the merger must be viewed from the standpoint of the Holding Company and not from that of any one subsidiary. If the assets and liabilities of the subsidiary are amalgamated with those of the Parent Company, it is clear that the reserve in the subsidiary company's Balance Sheet disappears, being off-set together with the shares acquired by the cost in the accounts of the parent undertaking.

"*Cost*" *includes Earnings of Subsidiaries up to Date of Acquisition.*

There is a further important point to be borne in mind in considering what is cost, viz. that all dividends received from any of the subsidiary undertakings distributed out of their surpluses existing at the time their shares were acquired must be deducted from the " cost " of the shares in the Parent Company's accounts.

When a Holding Company acquires the shares of a subsidiary concern it acquires, in effect, the surplus of assets over liabilities at that time. The price paid for the shares is assumed to have taken into consideration the then value of the assets as well as goodwill. Looked at in another way, the Holding Company bought and paid for any credit balances on Profit and Loss or other Reserve Accounts existing at the time, and it would obviously be improper for the Holding Company to treat these as its income.

A dividend paid out of these assets (or out of the reserves, whichever way it is regarded) is a return to the Holding Company of a portion of the assets acquired, or, in other words, a return of some part of the purchase money, and other things being equal, the shares of the subsidiary undertaking are in consequence of a less value than they were at the time they were purchased.

In the accounts of the constituent concern the surplus of assets might be represented by a balance on Profit and Loss Account or by reserve funds or surpluses on other accounts, and it would be within the power of each of the subsidiary companies to declare dividends out of any surpluses in whatever period accumulated. These dividends in the hands of the Holding Company are not earnings and must be credited in reduction of the cost of the shares acquired. In short, the Holding Company can only make profits and declare dividends out of the earnings of its subsidiary undertakings arising subsequent to the date of purchase. There is an illustration of this in the example in Appendix I in the case of subsidiary B., where it will be seen from the Balance Sheet of that company that a dividend was paid out of the profits earned before

METHOD I.—PRESENTATION

the date of purchase of the shares by the Holding Company, and, consequently, in the hands of the latter this dividend is a reduction of the cost and has been so treated.

It is of the utmost importance when examining a Balance Sheet of a Holding Company at any date that this point should be investigated. It should be seen that the total surpluses of all subsidiary undertakings, no matter on what account, in existence at the time of their purchase (after making due allowance for dividends since paid and credited in reduction of cost of shares as mentioned above) are still available to an amount not less than that total. If this is not so, it will be due to subsequent losses and reference must be made thereto on the Balance Sheet or in the auditor's report as is mentioned later.

In investigating the position, if, for example, an old reserve of one subsidiary company has been used and treated as income by the Holding Company, no exception would necessarily be taken to this provided it is offset by profits made subsequent to the date of purchase and not distributed in the case of other subsidiaries. That is to say the subsidiary undertakings should be regarded as a whole and not treated separately, subject, however, to the comments made later under the head of "Balance Sheets of Subsidiaries show Losses since Acquisition."

Difficulties occasionally arise in ascertaining the surplus of subsidiaries which from the standpoint of the Parent Company are to be regarded as capital, where negotiations for the purchase have extended over several months, and it is finally arranged to date the purchase back and base it upon the Balance Sheet at the close of the last financial year on the understanding that the earnings for the current period are to belong to the purchaser. Profits (or losses) will have accrued meanwhile, and it is then a question of fact how far, if at all, these profits have entered into the price finally agreed upon. It would not seem unreasonable to treat the earnings for the current year as income of the purchaser unless they have been included in the purchase price and consequently paid for by him.

Where interest is paid upon the amount of the consideration, as, for example, from the date of the prior Balance Sheet, it must, of course, be charged against the profits of the current year belonging to the purchaser.

Cases are not unknown where the articles of association of a company provide for the payment of dividends out of profits earned prior to incorporation, but it seems very doubtful whether such a course is legally admissible.

Is " At Cost " correct for Balance Sheet ?

How often one finds in a Balance Sheet the item Investments or Shares in subsidiary companies, or Holdings in and Advances to subsidiary companies " at cost." The question naturally arises: is this correct or can exception be taken to the item being stated " at cost." The answer to this can only be given after the facts of each case have been investigated and considered.

It is seldom that there are market quotations for the shares, and even if such quotations exist they are usually nominal, and it would hardly be fair to value the shares at these prices for the reason that no such value would probably be obtained for so large a block of shares at any one time, or, indeed, is it likely that they would be put on the market for sale. Recognition must be given to the fact that there are exceptions to this, and occasionally one finds that no difficulty would be experienced in disposing of a large block of shares privately to an interested party or undertaking at the nominal quotation or at almost any price within

METHOD I.—PRESENTATION

reason which might be asked. Where this is so the case has to be considered separately and dealt with accordingly. As a rule, however, market quotations are no guide for the purpose in view.

Another point which might be considered of importance is the income received from subsidiary companies. Assuming this income to be substantial, it may be regarded as sufficient yield on the total holdings to justify the " at cost " in the Balance Sheet. This is hardly the case, however, as naturally the income received would only be from those undertakings which are in a flourishing condition, while considerable losses may have been incurred by other concerns and not been provided for by the Holding Company.

A fairer way is to regard the subsidiary undertakings as if they were branches of the Holding Company, and from this point of view no exception would be taken to " at cost," provided it can be shown, as far as it is possible to do, that the position of the subsidiary concerns, taken as a whole, has not changed for the worse since they were acquired. For example, that losses have not been incurred other than those provided for by the Holding Company—that the total surpluses in existence when the shares were acquired are still available, and, generally, that so far as it is possible to say, the properties and other assets of the subsidiary undertakings have not deteriorated in value. At the same time the Holding Company could hardly be required to write down out of profits the cost of an investment in a subsidiary merely on the ground, for instance, that the land and buildings of a subsidiary by a general fall in values are worth less than when the business was acquired.

Examination of Balance Sheets of Subsidiaries.

This naturally involves an inquiry into the Balance Sheets of the subsidiary companies in order to obtain the necessary information. This is often rendered difficult by the fact that the auditors of the Holding Company are not necessarily the auditors of the subsidiary undertakings, and they have frequently to rely in such cases upon the certified accounts, supplemented by such other information as they are able to obtain from inquiries.

In this connection the following points should be borne in mind and investigated as to whether there are any errors of principle in the subsidiary companies' Balance Sheets looked at from the standpoint of the Parent Company or the consolidation as a whole, whether dividends have been paid by a subsidiary company without adequate provision for depreciation or other reserves, whether there are any contingent liabilities of the Holding Company for guarantees, such as of a note issue or bills of a subsidiary undertaking, and so on. It is not unusual to find that the dividend on the preference shares of one or more of the operating companies has been guaranteed by the parent concern, and if the profits of these undertakings are not sufficient to meet the dividend, the charge would necessarily fall upon the Parent Company. In the example in Appendix I, if the Holding Company had guaranteed the dividend on the preference shares of subsidiary A., the note on that Balance Sheet would not have appeared, as the dividend would have been discharged out of the Holding Company's profits.

Statement required of present Position of Subsidiaries.

The inquiry being completed, a statement should be prepared showing the exact position of the subsidiary companies, taken together from the standpoint of the parent concern, and, more particularly, with the object of seeing how far the position has improved or changed for the worse since they were acquired, that is to say whether, taking them as a whole, there are profits still undistributed or losses unprovided for by the Holding Company.

In the preparation of the statement adjustments will be necessary to make due allowance for minority or outside shareholders' interests, which is referred to later, and also to provide for all inter-company profits unearned.

In practice it will be found more convenient to prepare an amalgamated Balance Sheet of the Holding Company and its subsidiary undertakings because, as will be seen later, the position is brought more clearly into view. In fact, whether the amalgamated Balance Sheet is intended to be published or not, its preparation is invaluable to enable an auditor to get a correct view of the business as a whole and to decide what, if any, adjustments in the accounts are necessary or qualifications desirable before the Holding Company's Balance Sheet is certified. This is particularly necessary where there are a large number of constituent undertakings. In a case recently under the writer's review, over one hundred and fifty Balance Sheets were involved in the investigation of the Parent Company's accounts. This case was also complicated by the fact that some of the subsidiary concerns were themselves also Holding Companies, and the difficulties of the situation created by such a combination can be appreciated.

Inter-Company Profits and Balances.

With regard to inter-company profits as between one company and another, no exception could be taken to the transfer of stock in trade or sales to an allied company or the execution of capital works at a profit, but from the standpoint of the Holding Company, viewing the subsidiary undertakings as branches, it would not be justifiable to take credit for any such profits on stocks (or capital works) not disposed of to outside customers Similar remarks apply to such items as sales at a profit by one subsidiary company of goods obtained from another or interest on loans where the concern supplying the goods or charged with the interest is making losses which have not been taken up by the Holding Company. In all such cases the fact that such transactions between the companies may have been completed by actual payment does not affect the question of principle involved or alter the fact that appropriate adjustments should be made to set the accounts straight and to reserve where necessary for any such profits which are, in effect, unearned from the standpoint of the Holding Company.

All inter-company balances should be agreed in detail before the statement is completed. If there are items in transit which have not been taken up, whether by the subsidiary companies or by the Holding Company, they must be examined so as to ensure that any transactions between the companies directly affecting the Profit and Loss Accounts are properly dealt with and that profits made by one company at the expense of another are reserved for unless the loss to the other company is taken up in the same period.

If the subsidiary undertakings do not close their accounts and prepare their Balance Sheets at the same date as the Parent Company or as near thereto as to make no practical difference, the agreement of inter-company balances and the examination of outstanding items is obviously much more important. It also raises other questions involving possible irregularities which it is not the purpose of this book to enter into but which must be borne in mind.

Goodwill in " Cost " of Shares.

The statement or amalgamated Balance Sheet having been completed it will probably be found that the cost to the Holding Company of its interest in subsidiaries is not exactly represented

METHOD I.—PRESENTATION

by surplus tangible assets in those concerns; in other words there is a goodwill item in the cost. This will consist of the goodwill figures in the Balance Sheets of the subsidiaries, plus the premium paid by the Holding Company (or minus any discount received) after deducting any surplus or adding any deficiency in existence at the date the shares were purchased.

Is it necessary to deal in the Balance Sheet of the Holding Company with this item of Goodwill? It must be admitted that it is seldom any reference thereto is found, but it is suggested that it would give a clearer view of the state of the affairs if a note appeared in the Holding Company's Balance Sheet against the shares in subsidiary companies to the effect that the figure included goodwill to an amount specified.

If the assets and liabilities of the subsidiary undertakings are amalgamated with those of the Holding Company, the item Goodwill would necessarily appear in the Balance Sheet as such. Merely because the Balance Sheet of the consolidation happens to be prepared in some other form the goodwill of subsidiaries is allowed to be hidden away.

An auditor would, however, hardly be justified in qualifying his report if the directors objected to the Balance Sheet containing the note suggested.

Balance Sheets of Subsidiaries show Improved Position.

The most important figures in the statement are those showing what profits remain undistributed or losses unprovided for by the Holding Company. If the surpluses of the subsidiary concerns, taking them as a whole, have increased since the date of the acquisition of the shares, that is to say there is a profit in their accounts undistributed, then other factors remaining the same, the position has improved and, consequently, no exception would be taken to the investments in the Balance Sheet remaining " at cost."

It might be that the directors would wish to take up any undistributed profits of subsidiaries as an asset in the Holding Company's Balance Sheet and credit the amount to the Profit and Loss Account. If, as is assumed, the undertakings are not merely owned but effectively controlled, and the amount is properly disclosed on the face of the accounts, then no objection could be raised to this course provided always that any losses of other subsidiaries are reserved for. Where there is control which, however, is not exercised, it would appear inadvisable that undistributed earnings should be taken up, and, consequently, only dividends actually declared or proposed to be declared should be credited to Profit and Loss Account. In this country it is seldom that profits of subsidiary undertakings other than their dividends are taken credit for in the Parent Company's Balance Sheet, but if they are, care should be exercised to see that the amount does not appear under the general head of Sundry Debtors for the reason that it will not be collected unless the subsidiaries pay a dividend. It should be appropriately described as undistributed profit of subsidiaries and distinguished from any dividend declared or proposed to be declared by them which will be paid in cash in the ordinary course. This latter amount might reasonably appear under the head of Sundry Debtors.

It is necessary to mention here the possibility of abuse by allowing considerable profits to be accumulated year by year in the hands of subsidiary companies (paying only a small dividend or no dividend at all) and without any reference thereto in the Holding Company's Balance Sheet or Report. This would result in an understatement of the real profits of the consolidation, and unless the accounts of the subsidiaries are published or furnished to the shareholders of the Holding Company they would be entirely ignorant of the true results and the real value of their shares. From an auditor's point of view all such cases require special consideration, bearing in mind that the practice indicated if carried to excess may easily result in a point being reached where a Holding Company's Balance Sheet no longer shows the true and correct view of the affairs of the undertaking.

Instances will no doubt arise where a Holding Company acquires a subsidiary concern with a deficiency of assets, which latter is made good by profits earned subsequently. In the subsidiary company's accounts the profits would go to the reduction of the deficiency, but it is submitted that the Holding Company would be justified, if it so desired, in treating these profits as part of the current earnings of the consolidation as a whole and thereby increase the book value of the investment.

Inasmuch as the current profits would go to extinguish the previous losses, it might be contended that the Holding Company (even although it controlled the board of directors of the subsidiary) would not be in a position to withdraw the profits in the form of dividends as the current earnings would not become available for distribution until the deficit was eliminated. In practice, however, it is more than likely that any deficiency at the date of acquisition would be adjusted by a reduction of capital or by some other procedure, in which event the subsequent earnings would be immediately available for dividend purposes.

Losses incurred before the date of acquisition are as much capital as are profits earned before that date, and an appropriate allowance therefor would have been made in the purchase price. If these losses are subsequently wiped out, the value of the investment is correspondingly increased. As dividends paid out of surpluses at the date of acquisition are capital, so profits made since are revenue and could be so treated, though it is not suggested that they should be.

It is important to bear in mind that undistributed earnings of a subsidiary should not be declared as dividend by the Holding Company.

Balance Sheets of Subsidiaries show Losses since Acquisition.

It is now necessary to consider the position supposing the subsidiaries taken as a whole have changed for the worse: that is to say, there is a loss (after charging any dividends paid) which has arisen since the businesses were acquired.

It is submitted that this loss must be provided for by the Holding Company in its Profit and Loss Account and deducted from any amount standing as an asset in the Balance Sheet for " Holdings in and Advances to Subsidiary Companies."

If provision is not made for the loss the Balance Sheet of the Holding Company would not show a true and correct view of the state of that company's affairs, as credit would have been taken for dividends arising from flourishing subsidiaries, while no provision is made for losses incurred by others, all of which are for practical purposes branches of the same business.

This provision should be made even if in the accounts of the subsidiaries the losses have been met out of old reserves in existence before the shares were purchased, as these reserves are capital to the Holding Company and cannot be regarded by it as available to meet losses since acquisition. In such circumstances, until the old reserves of subsidiaries are made good, any dividends paid by them out of subsequent profits would be a return of capital to the Holding Company and, therefore, not available as dividend to its shareholders.

METHOD I.—PRESENTATION

In taking the subsidiaries as a whole and treating them as Branches as suggested it follows that losses incurred by some will be partly or wholly offset by any undistributed profits made by others. Where this occurs it is better that the subsidiaries having the profits should divide them and the Holding Company make the necessary provision for the losses of the others—in short, any offsetting should be done through the Holding Company's Accounts and losses of certain subsidiaries not provided for merely by allowing profits to accumulate with other subsidiaries.

In practice, some Holding Companies take up in their own accounts all losses made by constituent undertakings and not merely the proportion attributable to the number of shares held. This practice is undoubtedly in the right direction and should be followed wherever possible. Where it is done entries would probably be made to give effect thereto in the accounts of those subsidiaries whose losses would thus have been disposed of.

With other companies, however, it is not unusual to find considerable opposition to provision for any losses, and auditors are not infrequently told that they are really off-set by increases in the value of properties and are sometimes confronted with valuations to substantiate this point of view. They are finally told that in any event the directors do not propose to provide for the losses, and it is left to the auditor to decide what qualification he thinks necessary in his certificate to the Balance Sheet.

It is submitted that it is the auditor's duty to drawn attention in the most direct way to any such losses which are not provided for by the Holding Company. This is often set out as a note on the face of the Balance Sheet which, it should be mentioned, cannot be insisted upon, as the Balance Sheet is the directors' account. Failing this, reference must be made thereto in the auditor's report to the shareholders, and the amount of the loss should be mentioned.

This qualification should continue to appear until the loss is made good by subsequent profits or provided for by the Holding Company.

Even when a note appears on the face of the Balance Sheet it is a matter for consideration in each case whether the auditor's report should not call in question the value of the investments.

An auditor should not fail to draw attention to the losses even although he may be confronted with a valuation of the properties which shows that the losses might be wholly off-set by increases in value arising since the shares were acquired. There would be no objection to his referring to this when dealing with the losses. Increases in value existing at the time the shares were acquired are not, however, so far as the Holding Company is concerned, an off-set to losses of subsidiary companies made since that date as to the Holding Company these increases are capital and are presumed to have been taken into consideration in fixing the purchase price.

Illustrations in Appendix I.

Some of the points referred to above are perhaps better elucidated by reference to the example in Appendix I. The Holding Company has an interest in the subsidiaries as follows:—

Cost of Shares	£1,344,500
Deduct Premium on own Shares issued in purchase of Subsidiary A.	120,000
Net cost of Shares	1,224,500
Advances—	
Sundry Debtors	1,000,000
Bills Receivable	215,000
	£2,439,500

The final dividend of subsidiary B. at December 1921 is assumed to have been received immediately

METHOD I.—PRESENTATION

after the close of that year and is therefore left amongst the sundry debtors.

A summary of the Balance Sheets of the subsidiary companies shows Net Assets, apart from Goodwill of £1,057,942 after deducting proportion thereof to minority and outside interests, and the difference between this figure and the above total is made up of the following:—

	Company A	Company B (Incorporating C)	Company D	Total
	£	£	£	£
Goodwill—				
In Subsidiary Companies (proportion only) ..	90,000	73,578		
Excess of Cost over Nominal Value .		957,000	30,600	
Excess of Nominal over Cost ..	432,500			
	342,500	1,030,578	30,600	718,678
Capital Reserves being proportion of Surpluses in existence at date of acquisition of Shares, viz.: on Reserves and Profit and Loss Accounts ..	90,000	158,092	81,600	329,692
	432,500	872,486	51,000	388,986
Profit and Loss Account—				
Profits:				
previous periods			10,200	
this year ..		3,987		
Losses	1,009,125			
Stock Reserve ..		40,020		
Reserve Funds: this year	22,500	19,886		
	986,625	16,147	10,200	992,572
Total				£1,381,558

In view of these figures it would clearly be wrong to leave the item Holdings in and Advances to Subsidiary Companies " at cost " in the Holding Company's Balance Sheet.

First a note should be made against the items that the total includes Goodwill amounting to £388,986, although this could hardly be insisted upon if the directors objected, as has already been mentioned.

Then, as to the trading since the date of the acquisition of the shares, the net result so far as the Holding Company is concerned is a Balance of loss of £992,572. This loss must be reserved for in the Holding Company's accounts, which as they stand at present show a surplus on Profit and Loss Account of £802,500. If this is not done a reference to the amount of the loss not provided for would require to be set out on the Holding Company's Balance Sheet or in the auditor's report as previously mentioned.

An examination of the figures of the subsidiary companies puts an entirely different complexion on the Balance Sheet of the Parent concern. The surplus shown on that Balance Sheet, as will be seen, arises mainly from the dividends received from the flourishing company, viz.: Subsidiary B. amounting to £713,400. The next two items are of considerable importance, being the profit taken to credit from charges to subsidiary A. for interest on advances—£66,600 and for the profit on sale of goods obtained from A. amounting to £150,000.

It would clearly be improper to take credit for either of these unless provision is made for the loss incurred by subsidiary A. The loss of this company has been increased by the charge for interest on advances and probably also by a loss on the transfer of goods out of which the Holding Company made a profit. There is a similar item for interest charged against subsidiary A. in the accounts of B.

METHOD I.—PRESENTATION 43

Again in the Balance Sheet of A. there are stocks on hand purchased from B. at a large profit to the latter. From the standpoint of the Holding Company this profit has not yet been earned, and as credit has been taken for the dividends of B., amounting practically to the whole of the profits for the period, a deduction must be made for the Holding Company's proportion of B.'s profits on these stocks which amounts to £40,020.

The Holding Company's outside trading for the year has resulted in a loss of £100,000, and it is only by means of the dividends received from B. and the charges to A. that so large a surplus is shown.

An amended draft Balance Sheet of the Holding Company is set out in Appendix I giving effect to the adjustments already indicated, and this Balance Sheet shows a very different financial position from that set out in the original draft. Incidentally, it will be observed that the final balance on the Profit and Loss Account agrees with that in the Consolidated Balance Sheet referred to later.

At the same time it is obvious that this Balance Sheet by itself, legal though it may be, is at its best, a poor instrument wherewith to show the true position of the affairs of the Holding Company and its subsidiaries, or, in other words, of the consolidation as a whole.

General Remarks.

There are some who may say that in cases of this kind it would be sufficient if a reference is made on the Holding Company's Balance Sheet to the fact that some portion of the advances due from subsidiary companies is bad or doubtful. It is submitted that this is not enough and, moreover, it should be borne in mind that if a note of this character is suggested, it pre-supposes that the shares are worthless, because the first losses of a subsidiary company will fall upon the shares, and it is only after the capital has been exhausted that the advances which rank as ordinary creditors of the company are affected.

There are, of course, other factors to be borne in mind in considering the value of the interest in subsidiary companies in addition to those already mentioned. For instance, some of the properties may have considerably diminished in value since the shares were acquired, the shares may have been purchased at an excessive price having regard to subsequent experience, and for a variety of reasons and in the light of later information it may be obvious that " at cost " is an excessive figure for the Balance Sheet.

If an auditor is definitely of the opinion from any cause whatever that the interest in subsidiary undertakings is not worth the value at which it stands in the Balance Sheet of the Holding Company, even if all trading losses are provided for, it is necessary that his report should give expression to his view, and in such circumstances it would not be sufficient merely to state on the face of the Balance Sheet that the investments are included " at cost."

An auditor's duty in this respect is exactly the same as when dealing with the value of any other item in a Balance Sheet to which he takes exception.

It is not, however, suggested that the " cost " of an Investment must be written down out of profits merely on the ground for instance of a general fall in the value of land, buildings or goodwill of a subsidiary.

An auditor cannot be satisfied simply by an inspection of the share certificates of the companies owned. If he does not examine the Balance Sheets of the subsidiaries or does not receive all the information and explanations required in

METHOD I.—PRESENTATION

connection with them his report ought to state the facts quite clearly.

It must be admitted that every case which comes under review is not quite so easily dealt with as the one in the example. An auditor has often to rely upon information which to say the least is not full, and in all such cases he must decide for himself, after a careful study of the facts and circumstances surrounding each, how far he considers it necessary to carry his investigations so as to certify that the Balance Sheet shows the true and correct view of the state of the Company's affairs. He is entitled to take a reasonable view of the circumstances of each particular case and no precise rules can be laid down which will apply to all.

Chapter VII

METHOD (ii).—THE "LEGAL" BALANCE SHEET TOGETHER WITH BALANCE SHEETS OF SUBSIDIARIES.

To publish the Balance Sheet and Profit and Loss Account of the Holding Company as in Method (i) and to present simultaneously the separate Balance Sheets and Profit and Loss Accounts of all the subsidiaries.

It is not a very common practice to find the accounts of the constituent undertakings published along with the Holding Company's Balance Sheet. Indeed it would not always be practicable and might in some cases do harm, besides defeating its object by adding to the difficulties of shareholders and others reading the accounts instead of explaining a position already sufficiently complicated.

It is largely a question of numbers of subsidiary undertakings. If there are only two or three it is a useful practice to publish the Balance Sheets simultaneously if they admit of some comparison.

The best illustration is that of the large English banks, most, if not all, of which have allied undertakings either in this country or abroad carried on as separate companies and whose accounts are in some instances published along with those of the Bank owning them, partly no doubt for the perusal of depositors and others.

There are other companies where a similar procedure is adopted, but they are relatively few in number. Indeed, in the case of the large industrial undertakings where the investments in subsidiaries form a large portion of their assets and where the number of companies is large, it would serve no useful purpose to publish at the same time a number of separate Balance Sheets probably drawn up on different bases and taken as a whole, and as supplementary information would be unintelligible to the average shareholder and represent to him a confused mass of figures.

In such cases the Balance Sheets of the constituent undertakings would probably not be published at all except perhaps to serve some outside purpose such as with the banks to enable depositors and others to be assured of the stability of the allied undertaking. On the other hand, the presentation of the subsidiary companies' accounts is essential if there are ordinary shareholders whose shares have not been acquired by the parent institution, or if there are outside preference shareholders whose shares are not held by the Parent Company at all and who may be entitled to a copy of the published Balance Sheet. This also applies to debenture-holders.

If the subsidiary undertakings are carried on as public, as distinct from private companies, a statement in the form of a Balance Sheet would in any event have to be filed at Somerset House in the ordinary way.

Disclosure of Financial Relationship in Balance Sheets.

The publication of all the Balance Sheets at the same time has the advantage of disclosing the financial position of each subsidiary undertaking as a separate legal entity, but unless some essential detail is given showing the financial relationship between the Holding Company and its subsidiaries, it would hardly serve the purpose intended by the simultaneous publication, which is to give an idea of the financial position of the consolidation as a whole. For example, the Parent Company's Balance Sheet would require to show in detail the exact shares held in each constituent

METHOD II.—PRESENTATION

undertaking so that it may be seen how much of the total issued capital of each is held. Again, the inter-company balances between the Holding Company and its subsidiaries and also between the subsidiary companies themselves would require to be set out separately if they are sufficiently large to be essential to a correct understanding of the real financial position. This might be inconvenient and indeed dangerous for many reasons and especially bearing in mind the possibility of information being given to competitors. With many concerns it will obviously be very undesirable for information of this character to be published (as with subsidiary A. in Appendix I) and it is not likely that this method of presenting the accounts will be adopted in such cases.

On the other hand there are many cases where there are no inter-company balances, or where, being very small, they are comparatively unimportant and would not therefore be set out separately. Consequently the same objection to the presentation of the accounts simultaneously would not apply.

Where they are so presented, and information is given of numbers of shares held, it is doubtful if the position can be thoroughly understood unless the connecting link between the cost of the shares and the par value is supplied. For example, the cost will include the amount of any premium paid by the Holding Company for Goodwill and for any surplus profits, &c., in existence at the time. These surpluses will appear in the accounts of the subsidiary undertakings along with profits made since and be available for revenue purposes so far as they are concerned, but in the hands of the Parent Company they would go to reduce the cost of shares as already pointed out: in short, reserves in a subsidiary company are not necessarily available for dividend for the shareholders of the Parent Company. Again, information would also be necessary as to any surplus or deficiency arising on any revaluation of the properties and whether effect had been given thereto in the subsidiary company's accounts, thereby increasing or decreasing the reserves which so far as the Holding Company is concerned would be of a capital nature.

On the whole the arguments are against the presentation of the accounts in this way.

The " Legal " Balance Sheet as in Method (1).

If, however, this Method (ii) is adopted the Holding Company's Balance Sheet should be published in exactly the same way as in Method (i) and the remarks previously made under this head apply equally here. An auditor's requirements would not, it is submitted, be varied merely because the separate Balance Sheets of the constituent undertakings are also published at the same time. Although he might feel that shareholders could form their own opinion of the position of the subsidiary concerns it would not relieve him from the responsibility of reporting upon losses incurred and not provided for by the Holding Company to which reference has already been made.

Adjustments in Subsidiary Companies Balance Sheets.

So long as the constituent undertakings as a whole are making profits and paying dividends and the Holding Company does not take credit for more than its dividend, no difficulties arise, but the position is different if losses are being made which are provided for by the Holding Company or if the balance of any profits is taken credit for. An adjustment in the accounts of those concerns making losses or having a balance of profits would seem to be called for, transferring the loss or the balance of profit to the debit or credit of the Holding Company. If the Holding Company owns the whole of the share capital this would be in order. But, if as in the illustrations in Appendix I, the Holding Company does not own the whole of the shares and does not provide for the whole of the loss or take credit for the whole of the profit, but only for its proportion thereof, then an adjustment of the subsidiary company's accounts on the lines indicated above would not make the position clear for the reason that the balance then remaining in the subsidiary company's accounts, while theoretically representing the proportion of the loss or profit, as the case may be, attributable to the minority interests would, in effect, appear as apportionable to the whole of the capital. Unless, therefore, the whole of any loss made and not merely its proportion is provided for by the Holding Company, it would appear inadvisable to adjust the subsidiary company's accounts at all but to publish them with a note explaining that the Holding Company has taken care of its proportion of the loss shown.

Another item which requires adjustment is the final dividends proposed to be paid by the subsidiary companies, the whole or the due proportion of which has been taken credit for by the Parent Company. In the Balance Sheets of the subsidiaries the final dividend should be deducted from the balance of Profit and Loss Account as otherwise profits to the amount of the dividend will appear twice.

With many constituent concerns no special difficulties present themselves and the accounts can be published in the ordinary way without any adjustments. On the other hand, there are a number of companies whose accounts require special consideration and separate treatment and in respect of these no general rules can be laid down, but the points referred to here should be borne in mind.

Chapter VIII

METHOD (iii).—THE "LEGAL" BALANCE SHEET TOGETHER WITH A SUMMARY OF ASSETS AND LIABILITIES OF SUBSIDIARIES.

To publish the Balance Sheet and Profit and Loss Account of the Holding Company as in Method (i) and to present simultaneously as a separate Statement, a Summary of the assets and liabilities of all the subsidiary companies taken together.

This method of presentation has advantages over any other. It enables the Parent Company's accounts to be presented in the legal form, thereby showing what amount of money is invested in subsidiary enterprises. In addition, shareholders are furnished with a separate statement showing the total assets and liabilities duly classified of all the subsidiary undertakings and, usually, although not necessarily shown separately, the amount of the minority or outside shareholders' interest. On the assumption that the net total is linked up with the figures in the Holding Company's Balance Sheet it will also show the amount of goodwill, if any, in the cost of the shares and any surplus of assets belonging to the Holding Company and not taken up in its Balance Sheet.

There is one disadvantage in the aggregation of the assets and liabilities in this way in that it does not show how they are spread over the

METHOD III.—PRESENTATION

different concerns, and while this may not be of importance to a shareholder of the Holding Company, it may considerably affect a creditor of a subsidiary as the aggregated statement gives no indication whatever of the relative position of the individual companies. From the point of view of directors, the aggregation may be an advantage as the interests of the merger as a whole may be better served by the concentration of the operations in different places and under different control, e.g. production by one company and distribution by another. Comparison of results under such circumstances, or the publication of separate figures, might give an erroneous impression, as from the standpoint of the Holding Company they are regarded as one.

If this method of presentation is adopted, the Holding Company's Balance Sheet would be published in exactly the same form and dealt with in exactly the same way as indicated under Method (i) and the remarks under that head will accordingly apply here.

Summary of Assets and Liabilities of Subsidiaries.

It is only necessary, therefore, to deal with the statement setting out the summary of assets and liabilities of the constituent companies. Many of the points which have to be considered in the preparation of this statement also arise in the preparation of the consolidated Balance Sheet of the whole undertaking which is referred to later and accordingly it is not proposed to go into them in detail here. Among these points are: the possibility of subsidiary companies' accounts being prepared at different dates, the absence of any uniform classification of assets and liabilities, the values of assets of different concerns being set out on varying methods of computation, &c. A mere aggregation of figures from existing Balance Sheets without taking these factors into consideration, would serve no useful purpose and be of no practical value.

Again there is the question as to what holding would be considered sufficient to justify incorporating the assets and liabilities in a consolidated statement and the very important points arising on the ascertainment of the minority or outside shareholders' interests.

There are also questions relating to the elimination of inter-company balances and inter-company profits unearned which have to some extent been dealt with already.

It is as well to prepare the statement in columnar form as set out in the example in Appendix I. With a uniform classification of assets the work is rendered much easier.

Inter-company balances, including those with the Holding Company, should be shown under a separate head and must be eliminated from the final totals of assets and liabilities.

Final dividends of subsidiary companies paid since the date of the Balance Sheet should be shown amongst the liabilities, care being taken to set off inter-subsidiary company dividends, leaving an amount in the liabilities representing dividends due to minority shareholders and also the dividend accruing to the Holding Company which may have been taken up by the latter in its Balance Sheet.

It sometimes happens that one of the subsidiaries holds some of the Parent Company's shares, and in a statement of net assets of subsidiaries alone the shares will necessarily appear as an asset, although in a consolidated Balance Sheet of the whole undertaking they would be deducted from the issued capital of the Holding Company as explained later. If these shares have been acquired at a premium it is advisable, though

METHOD III.—PRESENTATION 55

not necessarily essential, that the premium figure should be treated as goodwill and only the par value shown amongst the assets as has been done in the example.

If the total goodwill of subsidiaries is treated as an asset (as in the consolidated Balance Sheet) and not merely the proportion attributable to the Holding Company, then it is not necessary to deduct from the minority shareholders' interest the proportion attributable to them as has been done in the example in the Appendix. Whichever way it is treated only varies the total amount apportionable to the minority interests and does not affect the final result of the amalgamated statement.

Surplus Assets Accruing to Holding Company.

The balance of the surplus assets represents the proportion thereof accruing to the shares belonging to the Holding Company. The difference between this figure and the cost of the shares is made up of two items, firstly, goodwill, and, secondly, current revenue balances representing any undivided profits (or losses) made since the date the shares were acquired and not yet taken up by the Holding Company.

If there are undivided profits the Parent Company might decide to leave them with the subsidiary companies, but if there are losses as in the example they should be reserved for by the Holding Company in its Balance Sheet. If not, attention would be drawn thereto by the auditors in the manner already outlined.

The figures in the statements will be more easily followed by reference to the corresponding figures in the consolidated Balance Sheet with which they are of course in agreement.

It will also be seen that the amount of the surplus assets including goodwill in the amalgamated statement agrees with the value shown against the item " Holdings in and Advances to Subsidiary Companies " in the Holding Company's amended draft Balance Sheet.

The only figures usually published with the Holding Company's Balance Sheet are those set out in the last column of the statement.

Chapter IX

METHOD (iv).—AMALGAMATED OR CONSOLIDATED BALANCE SHEETS.

To publish either separately or along with the Holding Company's Balance Sheet, as in Method (i), a Consolidated Balance Sheet of the whole undertaking amalgamating the assets and liabilities of all the subsidiaries with those of the Holding Company and a Consolidated Profit and Loss Account embracing the profits and losses of all the companies.

American Conditions.

In America the consolidated balance sheet is now almost universally adopted by companies whose interests in subsidiary companies form any considerable proportion of their total assets. The practice of issuing such a Balance Sheet began to spread at the time of the movement for consolidations about the end of the last century—a movement which culminated in the formation of the United States Steel Corporation in 1901. The consolidated Balance Sheet issued by that company has become in a large measure a standard for public corporations in that country.

In the first instance the practice had little support except from accountants. For some years the New York Stock Exchange required the filing of Balance Sheets of every individual company in connection with an application to list securities and either did not insist upon or declined to accept consolidated accounts. For many years now, however, the New York Stock Exchange has laid special stress on the necessity of filing consolidated Balance Sheets. The Federal Reserve Board of America has also, from time to time, expressed to the members of the System the view that the

Balance Sheet of a corporation having large interests in subsidiaries is not an adequate basis for consideration of an application for credit unless supplemented by a consolidated Balance Sheet or the equivalent.

The first legal recognition in America of the principal underlying the consolidated accounts is found in the tax statutes. The Federal Tax laws of 1917 contained no special provisions dealing with the case of corporations having subsidiaries, but the Commissioner of Internal Revenue, in the exercise of his power to prescribe regulations under that Act, required consolidated returns of the holding company and its subsidiaries in such cases, basing the regulation on broad considerations and principles and not on any express provision of the statute. The validity of this regulation does not appear to have been seriously contested by taxpayers in America.

In 1918 the whole American tax law was amended and an express provision for consolidated returns was enacted. Finally, in 1921, in order to set at rest any doubts as to the validity of the regulations issued under the Act of 1917, a clause was inserted in the Revenue Act of the year which reads in part as follows:—

> "Title II of the Revenue Act of 1917 shall be construed to impose the taxes therein mentioned upon the basis of consolidated returns of net income and invested capital in the case of domestic corporations and domestic partnerships that were affiliated during the calendar year 1917."

Accountants in America tell us that the case for the consolidated Balance Sheet is made out and that there is nothing further to argue about it on the question of principle. In any event, there and also in Canada consolidated Balance Sheets of holding companies are very common.

METHOD IV.—PRESENTATION

Position in this Country.

In this country the position is different and the consolidated Balance Sheet is the exception rather than the rule. The merits of the consolidated account are hardly known or appreciated here outside the ranks of accountants and the natural reluctance of the people of this country to change is too well known to require any comment. Perhaps, however, the greatest opposition to any but the most essential changes in the form of the published accounts comes from directors who are not all imbued with the desire of giving their shareholders as much information as possible, no doubt having in mind the necessity for avoiding disclosure of information which might conceivably be of use to competitors. Moreover, in view of the fact that the shares in the industrial concerns of this country are generally very widely distributed among a large number of shareholders, the call for the consolidated accounts has never been insistent. Shareholders perhaps can hardly be expected to know what form of accounts they require, but in recent years there has been a demand for more information concerning the position and results of subsidiary businesses. It is the duty of accountants to help them, but accountants cannot do it unaided as, after all, in this country it is the directors who prepare the published accounts and are responsible for the information given therein, although it is for the auditors to certify as to whether or not they are properly drawn up so as to exhibit a true and correct view of the state of the company's affairs.

Moreover, while there is no direct recognition of the consolidated account there is some indirect recognition afforded by the Finance Act 1915 where, in connection with Excess Profits Duty, it is provided that :—

"Where any company either in its own name or that of a nominee owns the whole of the ordinary capital of any other company carrying on the same trade or business or so much of that capital as under the general law a single shareholder can legally own the provision . . . . shall apply as if that other company were a *branch* of the first-named company."

No doubt it will be said that this clause was intended to deal more with profits, but the natural corollary to it would be the consolidated Balance Sheet as well as the Profit and Loss Account.

The consolidated Balance Sheet is seldom published alone in this country, no doubt for the reason that it is not regarded as the legal Balance Sheet. In cases where it is done, it is important that it should be appropriately described as a combined account with a note indicating what Balance Sheets have been amalgamated.

Some Advantages and Disadvantages.

On the whole it is better to submit the Amalgamated Balance Sheet as supplementary information to the so-called legal Balance Sheet of the Holding Company so that shareholders can see the financial position of the Parent Company in its relationship to shareholders and creditors and also the combined results as a single organisation.

This amalgamated account is essential if a shareholder is to be put in a position to form an opinion of the true financial status of the whole undertaking. It enables him to see the total interest (capital and revenue) accruing to minority or outside shareholders in the subsidiary concerns and what perhaps is most important of all, what surplus is available for the shareholders of the parent institution for dividend purposes. Further, it also shows what assets are available against the investments and how much, if any, is represented by

METHOD IV.—PRESENTATION

goodwill or even losses. There is also an advantage in the fact that inter-company indebtedness, shares, purchases, sales and dividends are eliminated and the figures shown on a net basis, while all profits and losses are automatically taken up.

Without some such consolidated statement it is extremely difficult to follow the figures from a mere perusal of the separate Balance Sheets, especially if the position is complicated by one of the subsidiary concerns being also a Holding Company.

On the other hand, there is a distinct disadvantage attaching to the amalgamated Balance Sheet in that it shows the value of shareholdings in constituent companies in the form of assets and liabilities irrespective of the fact that they are not legally the property or liabilities of the Holding Company.

Where, however, the Holding Company directs the policy and controls the operations of the constituent undertakings, it seems better to disregard the technical legal situation and to submit the substantial position which is to assume the Parent Company as owner of the assets and responsible for the liabilities and the interest of minority shareholders. Should the group of companies not be run as a whole certain of the subsidiaries might demand special treatment as it would hardly be reasonable to amalgamate the accounts under such conditions.

Preliminary Matters requiring Consideration.

Before coming to the consideration of the points arising in the preparation of the Balance Sheet, there are a few preliminary matters which it is essential to deal with first.

The Balance Sheets which are to be amalgamated should all be prepared at the same date. If some of the subsidiary companies prepare their accounts at different dates and different from that of the Parent Company's Balance Sheet it might be inappropriate to amalgamate them, but if no material change in the assets and liabilities had taken place in the interval, then possibly this fact could be ignored, provided it was mentioned on the face of the amalgamated Balance Sheet. In any event, there would probably be a number of outstanding transactions or items in transit between the various companies which would have to be investigated and properly dealt with in the combined account.

Another matter relates to the classification of the Balance Sheet items. Unless the assets and liabilities of all the companies are similarly classified an amalgamated account would hardly be intelligible and its value as a supplementary statement would be reduced accordingly. For instance, some companies may not have their fixed assets split up in their own accounts at all, as at the time they were incorporated they may have taken over some other business at a lump sum, and no attempt to allocate the purchase price between the different assets may have been made except where it was essential for domestic purposes. Obviously, before any useful consolidated Balance Sheet could be prepared, the assets of all the companies must be uniformly classified.

Again, inquiry would have to be made in order to ascertain if the values of the assets are computed on the same basis. With some of the concerns the assets may appear in their Balance Sheet at cost less the usual depreciation, while with others there may have been a re-valuation at some time and the cost figures adjusted accordingly, or the assets may be included on the bases of an estimate by the directors: in fact, very different bases may be adopted throughout the combine. To add to the difficulties, some or all of these values may be on an entirely different footing from that on

METHOD IV.—PRESENTATION

which the concerns were taken over by the Parent Company. When the shares were acquired by the Parent Company a re-valuation of the properties of some or all of the undertakings may have taken place which perhaps differs from the figures in the published accounts, and in fixing the purchase price appropriate allowances would no doubt have been made to give effect thereto. All these factors must be considered, as otherwise no useful purpose will be served by preparing a consolidated Balance Sheet.

Another important point is what amount of the ordinary capital in a subsidiary company should a Holding Company possess to warrant consolidation on the assumption that the ordinary shares carry control. It is impossible to give a general ruling upon this, as it must obviously depend entirely upon the circumstances, but effective control and direction of the policy of a subsidiary undertaking are important factors to bear in mind. While as a rule the assets and liabilities are not, in fact, amalgamated unless the Parent Company owns 75 per cent. or more of the ordinary capital, cases can be cited where a lesser holding warrants amalgamation. In the illustration in Appendix I the Holding Company purchased a bare controlling interest in Subsidiary D. amounting to 51 per cent. of the shares, but the facts here are deemed to warrant the inclusion of the assets and liabilities with those of the Holding Company. Each case is a matter for individual judgment, bearing in mind that the Balance Sheet should be properly drawn up so as to exhibit a true and correct view of the state of the Holding Company's affairs.

When it is decided not to amalgamate the assets and liabilities, then the shareholdings will appear as investments under a suitable heading in the consolidated Balance Sheet and care should be taken to see that any losses are provided for.

Effect of Amalgamation on Holding Company's Balance Sheet.

With these questions disposed of the work of amalgamation can be proceeded with, the effect of which is to eliminate from the Parent Company's Balance Sheet the item of investments in subsidiary undertakings and to show instead the actual assets and liabilities of the subsidiaries—in other words, treating them in exactly the same way as if they were branches of the Parent Company, with this difference, that in dealing with subsidiary companies a number of items will emerge and will have to be specially treated, which would probably not arise as between the Head Office and a branch of the same company. These will now be considered.

Goodwill and Capital Reserves.

The first and one of the most important is goodwill. In the consolidated Balance Sheet this will be made up of the goodwill, if any, of the Holding Company, together with any goodwill appearing in the Balance Sheets of the subsidiaries, also the premium paid or discount received by the Holding Company for the shares purchased after deducting the amount of any surpluses of subsidiary undertakings in existence at the date of purchase. Where shares are acquired at different dates the apportionment of the surplus at the date of acquisition must be made separately on each lot acquired.

If the amount paid for the shares exceeds the nominal value it is a premium and a discount if it is less. The premium, therefore, is the price paid for such proportion of the surplus (whether shown on the Balance Sheet or not) of assets over capital and liabilities of a subsidiary as accrues to the shares acquired, while the discount represents the proportion of the excess of the capital and liabilities over the assets.

METHOD IV.—PRESENTATION

If the cost of the shares exceeds the nominal value (as with subsidiaries B., C. and D.) it indicates there are surpluses in the subsidiary company's accounts which will require to be deducted from the premium as they were included in the price paid. If, however, there are no surpluses, or if there is a deficiency, then the assets or goodwill or both were considered at the time to be worth more than their book values, or perhaps one worth more and the other less, in any case, sufficient to show a surplus. But assuming the assets and goodwill were worth their book values only, it means that the Holding Company either made an unfortunate purchase or was prepared to pay a higher price to get control.

On the other hand, if the nominal value exceeds the cost (as with subsidiary A.) it indicates that there is a deficiency in the Balance Sheet of the subsidiary which will, in amalgamating the figures, be deducted from the discount, as allowance will have been made for this in fixing the price of the shares. If no deficiency appears or there is a surplus it means that the assets or goodwill were considered to be worth less than their book values, or perhaps one worth less and the other more: in any case sufficient to show a deficiency on the accounts. Assuming the assets and goodwill were worth their book values, it follows that the Holding Company has made a fortunate purchase, acquiring the right to more assets than it parted with.

By adjusting any increase or decrease in value of the assets against the premium or discount, the balance of the latter represents an increase or decrease in goodwill.

In practice all surpluses or deficiencies of subsidiary companies in existence at the date of purchase of the shares, whether on Reserve Fund, Profit or Loss or other account, or in respect of differences arising on the re-valuation of properties which it is decided to introduce into the Balance Sheet, are carried to a Capital Reserve Account. From the total is deducted any dividend which may have been paid thereout and treated as a reduction of the cost of the shares by the Holding Company as well as the pro rata proportion of the balance applicable to the minority shares.

Similarly the premiums paid for the shares and any discounts received are brought together under the general heading of goodwill and in the final Balance Sheet the Capital Reserve is deducted therefrom, thus leaving a net figure for goodwill.

This treatment is based upon the assumption that goodwill is shown as a separate item, but some concerns do not or cannot distinguish the goodwill from the general " cost of properties," and in such cases the adjustments referred to are shown under this general heading.

If the Capital Reserve should be the greater it would appear in the consolidated Balance Sheet as a surplus not available for dividend purposes and is sometimes referred to as "negative goodwill."

Some concerns do not set off "negative goodwill" arising on the purchase of one undertaking either against goodwill appearing in the accounts of the Holding Company itself or in the accounts of another undertaking in the same group or against goodwill arising from the purchase of the shares of another subsidiary. This appears unsound and it is more in accordance with the usual practice to set the one off against the other.

Minority or Outside Interests.

The next important matter relates to the ascertainment of the interest of the minority or outside

METHOD IV.—PRESENTATION

shareholders, which has to some extent been touched upon already.

The minority shareholder is usually the ordinary shareholder whose shares have not been acquired by the Holding Company and in addition to the nominal value of the shares he is entitled to participate in all undivided profits shown at any Balance Sheet date in whatever period accumulated and credit must be given accordingly.

Care is necessary in the actual calculations where a subsidiary company is in effect twice removed from the parent concern in that its shares are held by another subsidiary, generally referred to as a Minor Holding Company. This is illustrated by subsidiary B., which holds the shares of subsidiary C. in Appendix I, and where the outside interest must be calculated at two stages.

If a subsidiary concern issues new shares to the Holding Company, whether at a premium or not, a re-adjustment of the minority interest is necessary unless the minority shareholders take their pro rata share of the new issue.

With regard to the preference shares, the regulations of a company may make it necessary for the Parent Company to acquire at least a majority of these to get the control. This does not often happen, and it will usually be found that the Holding Company either does not own any of them or only owns a small proportion. Consequently the nominal value of any preference shares not owned by the Holding Company must appear as an outside interest, together with any unpaid cumulative preference dividend due to the fact that losses are being made by the subsidiary, as in the case of subsidiary A. in Appendix I.

Occasionally preference shareholders are entitled to participate in the surplus of assets on a liquidation, and effect is given thereto, in the case of subsidiary C. in Appendix I, where the preference shareholder is credited with the pro rata proportion of the surpluses shown after the payment of the amounts of the preference and ordinary capital.

As opposed to this it might be argued that it is not necessary in a consolidated Balance Sheet which represents the state of affairs of a concern at a certain date to reflect what might happen to a surplus in the case of the liquidation of a subsidiary, as it is hardly likely that a subsidiary would be liquidated as long as there was any surplus in which the Preference Shareholders had a right to share unless perhaps for the purpose of simplifying the internal organisation of the consolidation. A note on the consolidated Balance Sheet of the contingent liability to Preference Shareholders would then meet the case. The same remarks might apply to arrears of cumulative preference dividends.

Any outstanding debentures not owned by the Parent Company must appear as liabilities charged on the assets of certain of the subsidiary undertakings.

A peculiar point sometimes arises where a subsidiary company is making losses and where, in consequence, the minority shareholders appear to be charged with a proportionate part of a loss in excess of the nominal value of the shares held by them as in the case of subsidiary A. It might be argued that it is impossible for the minority shareholders to lose more than the nominal value of the shares subscribed for by them. This is undoubtedly the fact and were it intended to wind up the subsidiary obviously no proportion of any loss over and above the nominal amount of the shares would, in fact, be borne by any shareholder. As, however, was explained earlier in this book where the Parent Company considers it expedient to retain its ownership of the shares in spite of the losses, and in consequence it is not intended

METHOD IV.—PRESENTATION

to liquidate the subsidiary undertaking (subsidiary A. appears to fall within this category), it is necessary to view the position of the minority shareholder from the standpoint of the allocation of future profits. The minority shareholders in subsidiary A. would naturally be entitled to participation in future profits if and when their proportionate share of the loss now standing on that company's Balance Sheet has been extinguished.

This practice is not always followed on the ground that while the minority will share in profits the Parent Company will be obliged to make good or absorb the losses of the subsidiary to hold the organisation together. Where this is so, and the losses are fully provided for by the Holding Company, obviously there will be no need to charge the minority shareholders with any proportion.

Naturally if there is an uncalled liability on the shares the amount unpaid would be recoverable in a liquidation from the minority shareholder to make good his share of any deficiency of assets, so that in this case, and to this extent, the proportionate part of the loss on trading would eventually be recoverable.

Some concerns instead of showing the minority interests as a liability in the consolidated Balance Sheet only bring in the proportion of the assets and liabilities attributable to the capital held by the Parent Company. This procedure is not recommended and, moreover, is likely to raise other difficulties, for example, in the elimination of inter-company balances where a Parent Company has an amount owing to it by a subsidiary and only a percentage of the assets and liabilities of the subsidiary is taken up in the consolidated account, it would result in a difference in the inter-company balances which would have to be treated as an amount due from outside debtors in the consolidated Balance Sheet which would obviously be wrong.

Inter-Company Transactions, &c.

All inter-company indebtedness must be set off and not included in the assets or liabilities of the amalgamated Balance Sheet as it is the purpose of the amalgamated Balance Sheet to show the financial position of the affiliated group of companies to the public or outside world and not to each other. Reference has already been made to the importance of tracing any differences arising on inter-company balances and of ascertaining that they are properly dealt with in the Balance Sheet, e.g. goods shipped by one company and not received by another will have to be treated as stock in transit, and so on.

Final dividends payable by subsidiary companies will have been shown under Sundry Debtors in the Holding Company's own Balance Sheet. In the consolidated account the full dividend payable by the subsidiary must be deducted from the balance on the Profit and Loss Account and set off against the item in Sundry Debtors, the balance being the dividend due to outside shareholders which will be shown as a liability to them.

It is sometimes found more convenient to leave the preparation of the consolidated Balance Sheet until all inter-company transactions have been completed, items in transit taken up and the dividends paid so that the outstanding matters can be viewed in their proper perspective.

With regard to transactions in bills between the different companies the Parent Company may have drawn bills on a subsidiary and in the latter's accounts they will appear as Bills Payable while in the Holding Company's own accounts as Bills Receivable. In the consolidated Balance Sheet they must be eliminated altogether as inter-

METHOD IV.—PRESENTATION

company balances unless the Parent Company has discounted any of the bills, in which event the total discounted will appear amongst the liabilities. In these circumstances, the note as to Contingent Liabilities for Bills Discounted would disappear in the consolidated Balance Sheet as the actual liability is included instead.

Inter-company profits, whether on stocks, capital expenditure, &c., which at the date of the Balance Sheet were not earned, should be eliminated from the Profit and Loss Account and the assets reduced accordingly. This point has already been referred to earlier and it is only necessary to add that the minority shareholder has the right to consider that the profit has been realised, since the transactions have taken place with companies in which he has no interest. Only the Parent Company's proportion of the profit would therefore be reserved for.

If any of the profit was made before the shares were acquired no reserve is necessary.

An adjustment is frequently necessary not only in the figures at the date of the Balance Sheet but also to cover any profits in the stocks on hand at the commencement of the year which had not been previously adjusted. This means that the surplus on Profit and Loss Account at the commencement of the period must be reduced by the amount of any profit included in the stocks at that date and the profit for the period under review increased or decreased according as to whether the amount of the profit in the stocks at the end of the period was less or greater than that at the commencement. The stocks in the Balance Sheet at the end would be reduced by the reserve then required.

Fixed Assets.

In setting out the fixed assets of the consolidation it is necessary to inquire if the values shown in the Balance Sheets of the subsidiaries are to be brought into agreement with any valuations made at the date of purchase. If so, any surplus or deficiency shown is capital and care must be taken to see that it is so treated.

Subsidiary owning Shares of Parent Company.

A subsidiary undertaking may own some of the shares of the Parent Company which it acquired at a premium. In the consolidated Balance Sheet these shares should be treated as a deduction from the issued capital of the Parent Company and the premium added to the goodwill. Any sum receivable by the subsidiary on the liquidation of the Parent Company in respect of such shares would be returned to the Holding Company in the liquidation of the subsidiary except any proportion due to minority interest. Strictly, a reserve should be made to provide for the minority proportion of the Holding Company's surplus of assets over liabilities which accrues to that concern owning the Parent Company's shares in so far as it is in excess of the then book value of the shares held.

Contingent Liabilities.

With regard to contingent liabilities of the Holding Company towards subsidiary undertakings, it should be noted that they would not be shown on the consolidated Balance Sheet for the reason that the full liabilities appear instead. On the other hand, any contingent liabilities of the Parent Company or of the subsidiary undertakings to outside creditors would require to be set out in the usual way.

Foreign Subsidiaries.

Foreign subsidiary companies present special difficulties arising out of local conditions, apart from matters affecting fluctuations in exchange which it is not proposed to enter into in this paper.

Consolidated Profit and Loss Account.

In dealing with the Consolidated Profit and Loss Account care should be exercised to see that all profits of subsidiaries accrued prior to the date when their shares were acquired are transferred to Capital Reserve Account as not available for dividend or current revenue purposes. A deduction must be made for the proportionate part of current profits or losses attributable to outside interests according to the shares held and adjustments are necessary in respect of inter-company profits unearned.

Where the Profit and Loss Account is set out in detail inter-company dividends, purchases, sales and expenses would be eliminated.

Generally, it should be seen that any balance of profit (or loss) shown on the consolidated account, as available for dividend purposes, represents the profit (or loss) made by the Holding Company from the date it commenced its business, together with the proportionate share of all profits (after providing for share of all losses) made by all the subsidiary undertakings from the dates they were respectively acquired.

As already mentioned, the profits of Subsidiary Companies should not be declared as dividend by the Holding Company beyond the extent to which they have been actually distributed as dividend by the subsidiaries.

Consolidated Balance Sheet in Appendix.

Most of the points referred to are brought out in the consolidated Balance Sheet in Appendix I which is set out in full detail to show the workings and which should be studied closely by those desirous of knowing how the figures have been put together. It is only necessary to mention here that the final result of the profit and loss shown on the consolidated Balance Sheet is exactly the same as that appearing in the Holding Company's amended draft Balance Sheet.

Extract from Speech of Chairman of a Holding Company.

It will perhaps not be out of place here to quote from a speech recently made by the chairman of a very large industrial undertaking, which is also a Holding Company having considerable interests in subsidiary enterprises, as it seems to summarise the position very clearly :—

"The various constituent companies have, of course, continued to prepare their own legal Balance Sheets in the same form as existed when the exchange of shares took place at the formation of this company. These accounts obviously exhibit numerous differences of classification and also show the values of assets on widely varying methods of computation, different, too, in nearly every case from the uniform basis on which the merger acquired them. A mere aggregation of the existing Balance Sheets as they stand would, therefore, be very difficult, and of practically no value to anyone when obtained.

"But you will remember that, as a basis for the merger, a special uniform valuation of all the companies' assets and liabilities was undertaken on very conservative lines, and we continue to prepare on these lines since the date of acquisition a separate domestic Balance Sheet of our own for each company (based entirely upon the position then disclosed and adopted in each case). Any profit or excess of assets over liabilities, as

METHOD IV.—PRESENTATION

revealed by the special valuation at the merging date, has been put to permanent reserve, and of course, we regard ourselves as entitled to touch only profits made since that date, everything prior thereto being treated as capital as far as we are concerned.

" Now that we can get an aggregate of all these Balance Sheets—which as they are upon a uniform basis may properly be done—they represent the real state of the merger companies taken as a whole, and by watching the progress thus disclosed from year to year we are able to ensure not drawing upon the balance of assets over liabilities which existed (either as a carry-forward or reserve) when we purchased, and also to see that all losses since merging are fully taken into account against profits before our dividend policy is determined."

Chapter X

SOME NOTES ON TAXATION AS AFFECTING HOLDING COMPANIES.

This treatise on Holding Companies would hardly be complete without a few notes on taxation as far as it affects this class of undertaking, and the following are given in the hope that they will assist those who are specially interested in this side of the subject.

Income Tax.

In adjusting the Profit and Loss Accounts for the purposes of income-tax on profits, under Case I of Schedule D, income from investments will generally be excluded, either on the ground that it has borne tax at the source or that it is assessable under some other heading, e.g. Case III, IV, or V.

An important point arises when concerns are making trading losses, and where a company owns the shares in another company. If an individual carried on two separate businesses, or if one company carried on two or more businesses as separate departments, a loss incurred in one may be set off against profits made in another, under Rule 13 of the Rules applicable to Cases I and II of Schedule D. Where, however, the separate businesses are carried on by separate companies each company is a separate "person" for income-tax purposes, and in this respect income-tax differs from both corporation profits tax and excess profits duty. Hence, where a company owns all or a controlling interest in the shares of another company, and one of them is making losses, it becomes a question whether, with tax at the present high rate, it would be advisable to transfer the business of the subsidiary company to the Parent Company and carry it on as a department thereof, either winding up the subsidiary or keeping it in existence without its doing any trading.

In these days when losses on trading are unfortunately so common, it should be remembered that a trading concern can, under Section 34 of the Income Tax Act, 1918, set off a loss sustained in any year on its trading against any taxable income it may have (including its assessable profits on the business based on the average of the three preceding years).

If the trading losses for the year exceed the amount of the assessment on the business, the balance may be set off against income received from investments (e.g. subsidiary companies). Where, however, a business does not make a loss on trading in the year of assessment, but has an average loss on trading for the fiscal year, the income from investments must bear tax in the ordinary way.

A point which has particular reference to companies whose business is that of holding investments is the provision contained in Section 33 of the Income Tax Act, 1918. This section applies to any company " whose business consists mainly in the making of investments, and the principal part of whose income is derived therefrom." Where any such company claims and proves to the satisfaction of the Special Commissioners that for any year of assessment it has been charged to tax, by deduction or otherwise, and has not been charged in respect of its profits in accordance with the rules applicable to Case I of Schedule D, the company is to be entitled to repayment of so much of the tax paid by it as is equal to the amount of the tax on any sums disbursed as expenses of management for that year. A Holding Company, the whole of whose income is taxed either before receipt or under some heading other than Case I of Schedule D, might have difficulty in obtaining relief in respect of office expenses, salaries, commission, &c., were it not for this section. It must be borne in mind that the section applies to a variety of concerns as well as those to which the term "Holding Companies" is most commonly applied.

Another point frequently met with is how far a company is liable on profits made in dealing in investments. Are such transactions "capital" profits or "casual" profits, or are they part of the company's business and, therefore, assessable? It is a question of the facts in each case. The law in the matter was summarised by the Judge in the case of *Californian Copper Syndicate v. Harris*. After stating that the enhanced price obtained in the realisation of an investment is not assessable when what is done is merely the realisation or change of an investment, but is assessable when the change constitutes the carrying on of a business, the Judge continued: "What is the line which separates the two classes of cases may be difficult to define, and each case must be considered according to its facts, the question to be determined being, is the sum or gain that has been made a mere enhancing of value by realising a security, or is it a gain made in an operation of business in carrying out a scheme for profit making?" If the latter it is assessable.

Excess Profits Duty.

The capital employed in investments is usually excluded from the capital computations for excess profits duty purposes. A very rigid treatment of investments as being capital not required in a business seems to be contrary to the spirit of the excess profits duty and unfair in many cases, but it was nevertheless recently upheld in the Court of Appeal in the case of the *Commissioners of Inland Revenue v. The Gas Lighting Improvement Co., Ltd.*

A situation which commonly arises nowadays is where one company owns either all the shares or has a controlling interest in another company for the purposes of working the subsidiary company's business in conjunction with its own. It would seem equitable that in all such cases the two businesses ought to be taken together. If the subsidiary were a department of the Parent Company this would be the case, and it is submitted that the mere existence of a separate company ought not to prevent joint assessment.

The statutory provision, however, which is contained in paragraph 6 of the Fourth Schedule of the Finance (No. 2) Act, 1915, is that the assessment is to be a joint one only where two requirements are complied with : Firstly, where the company owns the whole (or as much as under the general law a single person can legally own) of the ordinary capital of another company, and, secondly, where the subsidiary company carries on the same trade or business as the Parent Company.

How narrowly this paragraph has been interpreted is seen from the case of the *Dunlop Rubber Co., Ltd. v. The Inland Revenue,* where a company had acquired the whole of the share capital of five companies with a view to ensuring the supply of raw rubber necessary to carry on its business. The Court decided that the business of growing rubber in the East was not the same as the business of manufacturing rubber goods from the raw material, and the companies had to be assessed separately. Hence losses made by one concern could not be set off against profits made by another, whereas if the Dunlop Company had bought the businesses from the five subsidiary companies and worked them as departments of its own business, even without putting the subsidiaries into liquidation, with exactly the same trading control and managed by exactly the same people, an excess profits duty assessment, based only on the net profits of the six businesses, would have resulted.

A very difficult provision is found in paragraph 8 of the Fourth Schedule of the 1915 Act. The idea of the Legislature appears to have been that a company dealing in investments should adjust tax on its profits or losses arising therefrom. If a company buys an investment which yields good profits, the price of the investment will presumably rise as a result of those profits, and the company holding the shares will make two profits, one on its dividends from the investment and one on the increase in the capital value thereof. On the other hand, if small profits, or no profits, are being made, the value of the investment may fall, and there will be a debit to Profit and Loss Account in respect of the depreciation in the capital value of the investment. This situation the Legislature seems to have felt itself called upon to obviate, and paragraph 8 (a) provides that any variation in the value of any of the investments which appears to the Commissioners of Inland Revenue to be due to a variation in profits, shall not be taken into account. The decision as to what has caused a rise in price of any particular investment is not a simple matter in the majority of cases.

A further difficulty in assessing a company (whose principal business consists of the making of investments) to excess profits duty in respect of dividends received is that those dividends may be from companies who have themselves borne excess profits duty on the profits in question. In other words, the dividends received are less by reason of excess profits duty having been paid. If the dividend itself is to be subjected to excess profits duty, the profits will be taxed twice over, and it can easily be seen that if the process is carried far enough the remaining profits ultimately approach vanishing point. On the other hand it is conceivable that in some instances the dividends may be more by reason of excess profits duty having been repaid. To provide against these anomalies paragraph 8 (*b*) provides that where income has been derived from profits in respect of which any payment or repayment of excess profits duty has been made under this Act, such deduction or addition shall be made in computing the profits as will make proper allowance for that payment or repayment of duty.

Fortunately for people concerned with the working of this regulation, the number of concerns to which it could be applied is found in practice to be very small.

Excess Profits Duty came to an end in the case of a trade or business which was commenced on or before 4th August 1914 on the expiration of 7 years from the commencement of the first accounting period, and in the case of any other trade or business (i.e. all new businesses) on 31st December 1920.

Corporation Profits Tax.

In adjusting the profits to corporation profits tax it is necessary to delete therefrom any interest, dividends, or income received directly or indirectly from a company liable to be assessed to corporation profits tax in respect thereof. That is to say, dividends received from British industrial companies will have to be excluded, but on the other hand income from any of the public undertakings which are excluded from the operation of corporation profits tax, such as gas, water, electricity and tramway undertakings, will have to be included with the profits, as also will income from foreign concerns.

One or two interesting points arise here. Interest on debentures received from an industrial undertaking will presumably be excluded, as debenture interest is not a charge in arriving at the profits of the undertaking in question, but interest, say, on a temporary unsecured loan will have to be included as it would be charged against the profits of the undertaking paying it. The only income from investments which can be excluded is that from companies liable to be assessed to corporation profits tax in respect thereof. In the case of a foreign company, a small part of whose business is carried on in this country and which has paid corporation profits tax in respect of that part and out of its general profits has paid a dividend which is received by a British company, the latter, presumably, has to ascertain whether the dividend it received has borne corporation profits tax in the hands of the paying company or not. How it is to do this is very difficult to say.

Where a company owns the whole of the ordinary capital of another (or so much as under the general law can lawfully be held by a single shareholder) the profits of the subsidiary may be merged with those of the Parent Company if an application is made by the principal company.

It is interesting to note the way in which the three principal taxes under British law apply to the situation where one company owns another. For income-tax they must be assessed separately. For excess profits duty they must be assessed together if they carry on the same business, but not otherwise. For corporation profits tax the matter is at the option of the taxpayer. If both companies are expected to make profits, separate assessments will, for corporation profits tax, be the more favourable to the companies, as, of course, there will be two allowances of £500 per annum. If, however, one company is making losses and the other profits, it is easy to see that it may be very much more advantageous to have a joint assessment. There is apparently no reason why, for corporation profits tax, the directors of the Parent Company may not change their minds on the subject from year to year if it be to their interest to do so.

Another interesting provision is where a company owns a controlling interest in and directs, or is entitled to direct, the management of any public utility company. Any profits derived from the public utility company are to be excluded from the profits of the Holding Company for the purposes of corporation profits tax, but would not whilst the utility company is itself exempt from tax be excluded from the profits of a company owning less than a controlling interest.

APPENDIX I.

	PAGE
HOLDING COMPANY'S BALANCE SHEET—	
Preliminary Draft	86
Amended Draft	88
SUBSIDIARY COMPANIES—	
A. Preliminary Draft	90
B. do.	92
C. do.	94
D. do.	94
PRELIMINARY SUMMARY STATEMENT OF ASSETS AND LIABILITIES OF SUBSIDIARY COMPANIES ONLY	96
DETAILED CONSOLIDATED BALANCE SHEET OF HOLDING COMPANY AND SUBSIDIARY COMPANIES	100

HOLDING
PRELIMINARY DRAFT BALANCE
(Drawn up to illustrate some of the

	£	£
SHARE CAPITAL—		
Ordinary Shares of £1 each	970,000	
Issued in exchange for Ordinary Shares in Subsidiary A.	30,000	
	1,000,000	
5% Cumulative Preference Shares of £1 each	600,000	
		1,600,000
5% FIRST MORTGAGE DEBENTURE STOCK		720,000
SUNDRY CREDITORS		245,900
RESERVE (Includes premium of £120,000 on issue of 30,000 Ordinary Shares in payment of 450,000 Ordinary Shares in Subsidiary A.)		500,000
PROFIT AND LOSS ACCOUNT as at commencement of year (after paying Final Dividends)	2,500	
Add—Net profit, viz. :—		
Sub. B. Interim Dividend £696,000		
Sub. B. Final Dividend 17,400		
Interest chgd. Sub. A. 66,600		
Profit on sale of goods purchased from Sub. A. 150,000		
930,000		
Losses on Outside Trading after charging Debenture Interest 100,000		
830,000		
Less—Dividend on Preference Shares .. 30,000		
	800,000	802,500
CONTINGENT LIABILITIES—		
Bills under Discount, Subsidiary A.	£110,000	
Guarantee of Debentures in Subsidiary A.	£250,000	
Guarantee of Loan in Subsidiary B...	£600,000	
		£3,868,400

NOTE.—On investigation the above Balance Sheet is as more accurately setting out the true position.

COMPANY.
SHEET, 31ST DECEMBER 1921.
points referred to in this book.)

		£
GOODWILL		150,000
FREEHOLD AND LEASEHOLD LAND AND BUILDINGS (*Less* amounts written off)		200,000
PLANT, MACHINERY, FIXTURES AND FITTINGS, &c. (*Less* Depreciation)		260,000
STOCKS		175,000
SUNDRY DEBTORS—		
Subsidiary A. Advances	1,000,000	
Subsidiary B. Final Dividend	17,400	
Others	110,500	
		1,127,900
BILLS RECEIVABLE—		
Subsidiary A.		215,000
INVESTMENTS, viz. :—		
Subsidiary Companies at cost—		
Subsidiary A.—25,000 Preference Shares at 10s.	12,500	
450,000 Ordinary Shares at 6s. 8d.	150,000	
Subsidiary B.—17,400 Shares at £75	1,305,000	
Subsidiary D.—20,400 Shares at £2 10s.	51,000	
	1,518,500	
Less Dividend declared and paid by Subsidiary B. out of surplus existing at date of purchase	174,000	
	1,344,500	
War Loans and other Investments	350,000	
		1,694,500
CASH AT BANK AND IN HAND		46,000
		£3,868,400

altered and an amended account prepared which is regarded (See amended draft Balance Sheet on next page.)

HOLDING
AMENDED DRAFT BALANCE
(As altered from Preliminary

	£	£
SHARE CAPITAL (Authorised and Issued)		
Ordinary Shares of £1 each	1,000,000	
5% Cumulative Preference Shares of £1 each	600,000	
		1,600,000
5% FIRST MORTGAGE DEBENTURE STOCK		720,000
SUNDRY CREDITORS		245,900
RESERVE		380,000
CONTINGENT LIABILITIES—		
Bills Discounted	£110,000	
Guarantees	£850,000	
		£2,945,900

* For details see Consolidated

COMPANY.
SHEET, 31ST DECEMBER 1921.
(Draft on pages 86 and 87.)

		£	£
GOODWILL			150,000
FREEHOLD AND LEASEHOLD LAND AND BUILDINGS (*Less* amounts written off)			200,000
PLANT, MACHINERY, FIXTURES AND FITTINGS, &c. (*Less* Depreciation)			260,000
HOLDINGS IN AND ADVANCES TO SUBSIDIARY COMPANIES (Goodwill included therein £388,986)			1,446,928
Investments (as on page 87)	1,344,500		
Less Premium Account	120,000		
		1,224,500	
Advances	1,000,000		
Bills Receivable	215,000		
		1,215,000	
		2,439,500	
Provision for net losses shown in Subsidiary Companies' Accounts per Summary Statement (page 99)		992,572	
Balance being surplus of Subsidiary Assets and Goodwill		£1,446,928	
STOCKS			175,000
SUNDRY DEBTORS			127,900
INVESTMENTS (WAR LOANS, &c.)			350,000
CASH AT BANK AND IN HAND			46,000
PROFIT AND LOSS ACCOUNT— Profit as at commencement of year		12,700	
viz.:— Holding Company	£2,500		
Subsidiary D. proportion	10,200		
	£12,700		
Net loss for year after deducting Debenture Interest and taking into account Profits and Losses of Subsidiary Undertakings	172,772		
Dividend on Pref. Shares	30,000		
		202,772	
			* 190,072
			£2,945,900

Balance Sheet (pages 107 and 109).

SUBSIDIARY

PRELIMINARY DRAFT BALANCE

(Drawn up to illustrate some of the

	£	£
SHARE CAPITAL—		
Ordinary Shares of £1 each	500,000	
5% Cumulative Preference Shares of £1 each	50,000	
(There are arrears of Preference Dividend amounting to £2,500)		550,000
5% FIRST MORTGAGE DEBENTURE STOCK		250,000
RESERVE—		
At date of Purchase by Holding Company	80,000	
Added since	25,000	
		105,000
BILLS PAYABLE—		
To Holding Company—of which held by latter	215,000 •	
Discounted by latter	110,000 •	
		325,000
SUNDRY CREDITORS—		
Holding Company loan	1,000,000 •	
Subsidiary B. Loan	101,000 •	
Other Creditors	290,000 •	
		1,391,000
CONTINGENT LIABILITIES—		
Bills under Discount	312,000	
Forward Contracts	2,150,000	
	£2,462,000	
		£2,621,000

HOLDING COM

25,000 Preference Shares at 10s. each		£12,500
450,000 Ordinary Shares at 6s. 8d. each		150,000
Purchase price to Holding Company		£162,500

"A."

SHEET, 31st December 1921.

points referred to in this paper.)

	£	£
Goodwill		100,000
Freehold Land and Buildings		400,000
Plant and Machinery (*Less* Depreciation)		500,000
Stocks (Includes £201,250 purchased from Subsidiary B. this year at a profit to B. of 20% or £40,250)		315,000
Sundry Debtors—		
Subsidiary C.	2,500	
Others	171,500	
		174,000
Bills Receivable		25,000
Cash at Bank and in Hand		7,000
Profit and Loss Account—		
Profit at date of Purchase..	20,000	
Net Loss since after charging Debenture Interest and Transfer to Reserve	1,120,000	
		1,100,000
		£2,621,000

PANY ACQUIRED.

Preference Shares acquired for cash	12,500
Purchase price of Ordinary Shares satisfied by issue of 30,000 Ordinary Shares in Holding Company of a market value of £5 each	£150,000
	£162,500

SUBSIDIARY

PRELIMINARY DRAFT BALANCE

(Drawn up to illustrate some of the

	£	£
SHARE CAPITAL—		
17,500 Shares of £10 each..		175,000
LOAN FROM BANKERS (SECURED)		600,000
SUNDRY CREDITORS—		
Subsidiary C.	1,000	
Others	138,000	
		139,000
RESERVE—		
At date of Purchase by Holding Company ..	30,000	
Added since	20,000	
		50,000
PROFIT AND LOSS ACCOUNT—		
At date of Purchase by Holding Company ..	200,000	
Less Dividend since paid thereout	175,000	
	25,000	
Net Profit since— (Includes—Dividend to come from Subsidiary C., £18,200 Interest on Loan to Subsidiary A., £10,000) ..	741,250	
	766,250	
Less—Transferred to Reserve £20,000 Interim Dividend paid November, 400% 700,000		
	720,000	
		46,250
		£1,010,250

Holding Company acquired 17,400

"B."

SHEET, 31ST DECEMBER 1921.
points referred to in this book.)

	£	£
FREEHOLD BUILDINGS		150,000
PLANT AND MACHINERY (*Less* Depreciation)		265,000
INVESTMENTS AT COST—		
2,600 Ordinary Shares of £10 each in Subsidiary C.	80,000	
80,000 Ordinary Shares of £1 each in Holding Company	100,000	
		180,000
STOCKS		202,750
SUNDRY DEBTORS—		
Subsidiary A. Loan	101,000	
Subsidiary C. Final Dividend ..	18,200	
Others	64,800	
		184,000
CASH AT BANK		28,500
		£1,010,250

Shares at £75 each = £1,305,000.

SUBSIDIARY
PRELIMINARY DRAFT BALANCE
(Drawn up to illustrate some of the

	£	£
SHARE CAPITAL—		
2,600 Ordinary Shares of £10 each..	26,000	
1,400 10% Preference Shares of £10 each	14,000	
		40,000
(The Preference Shareholders are entitled under Company's Articles to share *pro rata* with Ordinary Shareholders in Surplus Assets on a winding up)		
4½% 1ST MORTGAGE DEBENTURES ..		210,000
SUNDRY CREDITORS—		
Subsidiary A. ..	2,500	
Others ..	129,000	
		131,500
RESERVE—		
At date of Purchase by Subsidiary B.		40,000
PROFIT AND LOSS ACCOUNT—		
At date of Purchase by Subsidiary B.	120,000	
Add : Net profit since after charging Debenture Interest	20,000	
		140,000
		£561,500

Subsidiary B. owns all Ordinary

SUBSIDIARY
PRELIMINARY DRAFT BALANCE
(Drawn up to illustrate some of the

	£
SHARE CAPITAL—	
40,000 Shares of £1 each ..	40,000
SUNDRY CREDITORS ..	110,000
RESERVE—	
At date of Purchase by Holding Company ..	160,000
PROFIT AND LOSS ACCOUNT—	
As last Balance Sheet (since date of Purchase) ..	20,000
	£330,000

Holding Company purchased bare controlling interest

" C."
SHEET, 31ST DECEMBER 1921.
points referred to in this book.)

	£	£
LEASEHOLD BUILDINGS (*Less* amounts written off)		50,000
MACHINERY AND FIXTURES (*Less* Depreciation)		130,000
STOCKS		150,000
SUNDRY DEBTORS—		
Subsidiary B.	1,000	
Others	219,000	
		220,000
CASH AT BANK AND IN HAND		11,500
		£561,500

Shares at cost of £80,000.

" D."
SHEET, 31ST DECEMBER 1921.
points referred to in this book.)

	£
MACHINERY AND PLANT (*Less* Depreciation) ..	140,000
STOCKS	130,000
SUNDRY DEBTORS	45,000
CASH AT BANK	15,000
	£330,000

(51%) 20,400 shares at £2 10s. each = £51,000.

SUBSIDIARY

PRELIMINARY SUMMARY STATEMENT OF VIEW OF HOLD

FREEHOLD AND LEASEHOLD LAND AND BUILDINGS—
(*Less* amounts written off) .. ..
PLANT, MACHINERY, FIXTURES & FITTINGS &c.—
(*Less* Depreciation) .. ..

INVESTMENTS (IN Holding Company at par value) .. ..

STOCKS .. ..

SUNDRY DEBTORS .. ..

BILLS RECEIVABLE .. ..

CASH AT BANK AND IN HAND .. ..

Associated Companies .. ..

Less :
    DEBENTURES .. ..

    LOANS .. ..

    SUNDRY CREDITORS AND BILLS PAYABLE .. .. ..

    FINAL DIVIDENDS .. ..

    Associated Companies .. ..

        Do.   Profit on Stocks held .. ..

                                    Carry forward

COMPANIES.

ASSETS AND LIABILITIES FROM POINT OF ING COMPANY.

				Total	
A.	B.	C.	D.	Inter Co. Balances	Net
£ 400,000	£ 150,000	£ 50,000	£	£	£ 600,000
500,000	265,000	130,000	140,000		1,035,000
	80,000				80,000
315,000	202,750	150,000	130,000	40,020	757,730
171,500	64,800	219,000	45,000		500,300
25,000					25,000
7,000	28,500	11,500	15,000		62,000
2,500	119,200	1,000		122,700	
1,421,000	910,250	561,500	330,000	162,720	3,060,030
250,000		210,000			460,000
	600,000				600,000
400,000	138,000	129,000	110,000		777,000
	17,500	19,600		18.200	18,900
1,316,000	1,000	2,500		1,319,500	
	40,020				40,020
545.000	113,730	200,400	220,000	1,215,000	1,204,130

Subsidiary

Brought forward
PROPORTION ACCRUING TO OUTSIDE SHAREHOLDERS—
   Ordinary and Preference Shares .. ..
   Proportion of Reserves, Profit and Loss Balances and Final
      Dividends (for details see Consolidated Balance
      Sheet) .. ..
   Less : Goodwill attributable to Outside Shareholders ..

BALANCE OF SURPLUS ASSETS NOT INCLUDING GOODWILL ..

GOODWILL (for details see Consolidated Balance Sheet)—
   Subsidiary Companies (proportion only) .. .. ..
   Excess of Cost of Shares over nominal value .. ..
   Excess of nominal value over cost of shares .. .. ..

      Less : Surpluses in existence at date of acquisition of Shares,
         viz. : Reserves and Profit and Loss Balances.. ..

     HOLDING COMPANY'S BALANCE SHEET SHOWS—
       Subsidiary Companies cost of Shares .. ..
         Less : Premium on Shares issued on purchase
           of Subsidiary A. .. ..

       Advances to Subsidiary companies—
         Sundry Debtors .. ..
         Bills Receivable .. ..
      BALANCE CONSISTS OF—
       Revenue Balances (for details see Consolidated
       Balance Sheet).
         Profits (previous period) .. .. ..
         Profits (this year) .. ..
         Losses .. ..
         Stock Reserve .. ..
       Reserve Accounts .. ..

Companies—(contd.).

545,000	113,730	200,400	220,000	*1,215,000*	1,204,130
75,000	1,000	14,000	19,600		
loss 98,375	1,045	56,140	88,200		
10,000	422				
33,375	1,623	70,140	107,800		146,188
511,625	112,107	130,260	112,200	*1,215,000*	1,057,942
	(incorporating C)				
90,000	73,578		30,600		
432,500	957,000				
342,500	1,030,578		30,600	718,678	
90,000	*158,092*		*81,600*	*329,692*	
432,500	872,486		51,000		388,986
	TOTAL (*See Amended Balance Sheet*)				.. £1,446,928
				1,344,500	
				120,000	
				1,224,500	
			1,000,000		
			215,000	1,215,000	
				2,439,500	
			10,200		
	3,987				
1,009,125					
	40,020				
22,500	*19,886*				
				(*Loss*)	
£986,625	£16,147		£10,200	*£992,572*	£1,446,928

HOLDING COMPANY AND
DETAILED CONSOLIDATED BALANCE SHEET

		£	£
ORDINARY SHARES OF £1 EACH		1,000,000	
5% CUMULATIVE PREFERENCE SHARES OF £1 EACH		600,000	
		1,600,000	
Less : Ordinary Shares held by Sub. B.		80,000	
			1,520,000
5% 1ST MORTGAGE DEBENTURE STOCK			720,000
SUBSIDIARY COMPANIES. (Capital held by Outside Shareholders)			
ORDINARY SHARES.			
Subsidiary A. 50,000 Shares of £1 each	50,000		
Subsidiary B. 100 Shares of £10 each	1,000		
Subsidiary D. 19,600 Shares of £1 each	19,600		
		70,600	
PREFERENCE SHARES.			
Subsidiary A. 25,000 5% Cumulative Preference Shares of £1 each	25,000		
Subsidiary C. 1,400 10% Preference Shares of £10 each	14,000		
		39,000	
		109,600	
DEBENTURES.			
Subsidiary A. 5% 1st Mortgage Debenture Stock (Secured on Assets of book value of £1,421,000)	250,000		
Subsidiary C. 4½% 1st Mortgage Debentures (Secured on Assets of book value of £561,500)	210,000		
		460,000	
			569,600
	Forward		2,809,600

ITS SUBSIDIARY COMPANIES.
TO SHOW WORKINGS, 31ST DECEMBER 1921.

		£	£
GOODWILL.			
Holding Company		150,000	
Subsidiary A.		100,000	
Add : Excess of cost of shares of Subsidiary Companies over their Nominal value, viz. :—			
Subsidiary B. Cost 1,305,000			
Less : Dividend (see Capital Reserve per contra) .. 174,000			
1,131,000			
Nominal 174,000			
	957,000		
Subsidiary C. Cost 80,000			
Nominal 26,000			
	54,000		
Subsidiary D. Cost 51,000			
Nominal 20,400			
	30,600		
Excess of cost of Shares of Holding Company over their Nominal Value, viz.:			
Subsidiary B. Cost 100,000			
Nominal 80,000			
	20,000		
		1,061,600	
		1,311,600	
Deduct.			
Excess of Nominal Values over Cost, viz. :—			
Subsidiary A.			
Ordinary Shares			
Nominal .. 450,000			
Cost 150,000			
Less: Premium on Shares issued 120,000 30,000	420,000		
Preference Shares			
Nominal .. 25,000			
Cost .. 12,500			
	12,500		
		432,500	
Note : In the published account the Capital Reserve per contra would be deducted from the above total.			879,100
	Forward		879,100

Holding Company and its

	Forward ..			2,809,600

PROPORTION OF RESERVES AND PROFIT AND LOSS BALANCES OF SUBSIDIARY COMPANIES DUE TO OUTSIDE SHAREHOLDERS.

Subsidiary A.			
Preference Shareholders Arrears of Preference Dividend		1,250	
Ordinary Shareholders			
Reserve (see below) ..	2,500		
Capital Reserve (see below)	10,000		
Profit & Loss (see contra) .. .. *Loss*	112,125		
		99,625	
Subsidiary B.			
Reserve (see below) ..	114		
Capital Reserve (see below)	908		
Profit & Loss (see contra)	21		
Profit & Loss Sub. C. (see contra)	2		
		1,045	
Subsidiary C.			
Capital Reserve (see below)	56,000		
Profit & Loss (see contra)	140		
		56,140	
Subsidiary D.			
Capital Reserve (see below)	78,400		
Profit and Loss (see contra)	9,800		
		88,200	
			47,010

CAPITAL RESERVE.
Representing proportion of Reserves and Profit & Loss Balances of subsidiary Companies at date of their purchase, viz. :—

Subsidiary A.			
Reserve	80,000		
Profit & Loss	20,000		
	100,000		
Less : Proportion applicable to Outside Shareholders, viz. : 50,000 / 500,000 ..	10,000		
		90,000	

Forward		90,000	2,856,610

Subsidiary Companies—(*contd.*).

Forward			. 879,100

FREEHOLD AND LEASEHOLD LAND AND BUILDINGS (less amounts written off)

Holding Company	200,000	
Subsidiary A.	400,000	
Subsidiary B.	150,000	
Subsidiary C.	50,000	
Subsidiary D.	—	
		800,000

PLANT, MACHINERY, FIXTURES AND FITTINGS, &c. (less depreciation)

Holding company	260,000	
Subsidiary A.	500,000	
Subsidiary B.	265,000	
Subsidiary C.	130,000	
Subsidiary D.	140,000	
		1,295,000

STOCKS.

Holding Company		175,000	
Subsidiary A.	315,000		
Less : Inter Company Profit, viz. :—			
$\frac{174}{175}$ of £40,250	40,020		
		274,980	
Subsidiary B.		202,750	
Subsidiary C.		150,000	
Subsidiary D.		130,000	
			932,730

SUNDRY DEBTORS.

Holding Company		1,127,900		
Less : Subsidiary A.	1,000,000			
Subsidiary B. Final Dividend	17,400	1,017,400		
			110,500	
Subsidiary A.		174,000		
Less : Subsidiary C.		2,500		
			171,500	
Subsidiary B.		184,000		
Less : Subsidiary A.	101,000			
Subsidiary C. Final Dividend	18,200	119,200		
			64,800	
Subsidiary C.		220,000		
Less : Subsidiary B.		1,000		
			219,000	
Subsidiary D.			45,000	
				610,800

Forward		4,517,630

Holding Company and its

Forward		90,000	2,856,610
Subsidiary B.			
Reserve	30,000		
Profit & Loss (after deducting Dividend £175,000 see contra)	25,000		
Surplus of Subsidiary C. (as below)	104,000		
	159,000		
Less : Proportion applicable to Outside Shareholders, viz.: $\frac{1,000}{175,000}$	908	158,092	
Subsidiary C.			
Reserve	40,000		
Profit and Loss	120,000		
	160,000		
Less : Proportion applicable to Outside Preference Shareholders, viz.: $\frac{14,000}{40,000}$	56,000		
Balance applicable to Ordinary Shareholders Subsidiary B, viz.: $\frac{26,000}{40,000}$ carried above	104,000		
Subsidiary D.			
Reserve	160,000		
Less : Proportion applicable to Outside Shareholders, viz.: $\frac{19,600}{40,000}$	78,400	81,600	329,692

NOTES:—

(1) Any increase or decrease arising on Revaluation of properties made at the time the concerns were acquired would if brought into the Balance Sheet be added to or deducted from the above Capital Reserves and the Assets adjusted accordingly.

(2) In the published accounts the total of Capital Reserve would be deducted from Goodwill per contra.

Forward		3,186,302

Subsidiary Companies—(contd.).

Forward				4,517,630
BILLS RECEIVABLE.				
Holding Company			215,000	
Subsidiary A.			25,000	
			240,000	
Less : Subsidiary A. Bills Payable			215,000	
				25,000
INVESTMENTS.				
Holding Company		1,694,500		
Subsidiary B.		180,000		
			1,874,500	
Less : Subsidiary Companies Total			1,524,500	
				350,000
CASH AT BANK AND IN HAND.				
Holding Company			46,000	
Subsidiary A.			7,000	
Subsidiary B.			28,500	
Subsidiary C.			11,500	
Subsidiary D.			15,000	
				108,000
PROFIT AND LOSS ACCOUNT BALANCES.				
Holding Company—Profit			802,500	
Subsidiary A.—Loss		1,100,000		
Add : Balance at date of purchase transferred to Capital Reserve		20,000		
		1,120,000		
Arrears of Cumulative Preference Dividend due to Outside Preference Shareholders $\frac{25,000}{50,000} \times 2,500$		1,250		
		1,121,250		
Less : Proportion applicable to Outside Shareholders $\frac{50,000}{500,000}$		112,125	1,009,125	
Subsidiary B.—Profit		46,250		
Less : Balance at date of purchase transferred to Capital Reserve .. 25,000				
Final Dividend (since paid) .. 17,500		42,500		
		3,750		
Forward	..	3,750	206,625	5,000,630

Holding Company and its

Forward				3,186,302
LOANS FROM BANKERS.				
Subsidiary B.				600,000
(Secured on Assets of Book Value of £1,010,250)				
SUNDRY CREDITORS.				
Holding Company			245,900	
Subsidiary A.		1,391,000		
Less: To Holding Company.. ..1,000,000				
To Subsidiary B. 101,000	1,101,000			
			290,000	
Subsidiary B. .. 139,000				
Less: To Subsidiary C. 1,000	138,000			
Final Dividend .. 17,500				
Less: Received by Holding Co. .. 17,400	100			
			138,100	
Subsidiary C. 131,500				
Less: To Subsidiary A. 2,500				
	129,000			
Final Dividend .. 19,600				
Less: Received by Subsidiary B. .. 18,200	1,400			
			130,400	
Subsidiary D.			110,000	
				914,400
BILLS PAYABLE.				
Subsidiary A.			325,000	
Less: Held by Holding Co.			215,000	
				110,000
RESERVES.				
Subsidiary A.	105,000			
Less: Balance of Reserve when interest in Company was purchased transferred to Capital Reserve ..	80,000			
	25,000			
Less: Proportion applicable to outside Shareholders				
$\frac{50,000}{500,000}$	2,500			
			22,500	
	Forward ..		22,500	4,810,702

Subsidiary Companies—(contd.)

Forward		3,750	206,625	5,000,630
Less : Proportion applicable to Outside Shareholders, viz. :—				
$\frac{1}{175}$		21		
			3,729	
Inter Company Profit on Stocks on hand in Subsidiary A. now written back, viz. :—				
$\frac{174}{175}$ of £40,250			40,020	
Subsidiary C.—Profit		140,000		
Less : Balance at date of purchase transferred to Capital Reserve ..	120,000			
Final Dividends (since paid) ..	19,600			
		139,600		
		400		
Less : Proportion applicable to Preference Shareholders, viz. :—				
$\frac{14}{40}$		140		
		260		
Less : Proportion applicable to Outside Shareholders, viz. :—				
$\frac{1}{175}$		2	258	
Subsidiary D.—Profit		20,000		
Less : Proportion applicable to Outside Shareholders, viz. :—				
$\frac{196}{400}$		9,800	10,200	
			232,458	
Deduct : Reserves Sub. A. and B. (per contra)			42,386	
				190,072
Forward				5,190,702

Holding Company and its

		Forward ..	22,500	4,810,702
Subsidiary B.		50,000		
Less : Balance of Reserve when interest in Company was purchased transferred to Capital Reserve ..		30,000		
		20,000		
Less : Proportion applicable to Outside Shareholders, viz. :—				
$\dfrac{1}{175}$		114		
			19,886	
Subsidiary C.		40,000		
Less : Balance of Reserve when interest in Company was purchased transferred to Capital Reserve ..		40,000	—	
Subsidiary D.		160,000		
Less : Balance of Reserve when interest in Company was purchased transferred to Capital Reserve ..		160,000	—	
Transferred to Profit & Loss Account (per contra)			£42,386	
Holding Company			500,000	
Less : Premium on Shares deducted from Goodwill (per contra)			120,000	
				380,000
CONTINGENT LIABILITIES.				
Subsidiary A.				
Bills under Discount			£312,000	
Forward Contracts			£2,150,000	
Holding Company.				
Bills under discount ..		£110,000	Not required as now shown under liabilities above.	
Guarantee of Debentures in Subsidiary A.		£250,000		
Guarantee of Loan in Subsidiary B.		£600,000		
				£5,190,702

Subsidiary Companies—*(contd.)*.

			Forward		5,190,702
Or thus:—					

BALANCE OF PROFIT AT COMMENCEMENT OF
YEAR :—

Holding Company			2,500		
Subsidiary D.		20,000			
Less : Proportion applicable to Outside Shareholders viz. : $\frac{196}{400}$		9,800			
			10,200		
				12,700	

Loss for year, viz. :
Subsidiary A.—
  Loss   *1,096,250*
  Less: Proportion accruing to Outside Shareholders
  1-10th   *109,625*
                        986,625 *Loss*

Profits for year, viz :
Subsidiary B.   741,250
  Less : Proportion accruing to Outside Shareholders
  1-175th   4,235
  Profit on Stocks held by Sub. A. written back 40,020   44,255   696,995

Subsidiary C.   20,000
  Less : Final Dividends   19,600
  Proportion accruing to Preference Shareholders   140
              19,740
Proportion accruing to Outside Shareholders of Subsidiary B. viz.:
1-175th   ..   2   19,742   258

Holding Company   800,000
  Less: Dividends of Subsidiary Companies   ..   713,400   86,600

			Net Loss	..	202,772
Balance as above	..	..	..		£190,072

					£5,190,702

APPENDIX I.

Examples of Actual Published Balance Sheets.

The following are examples of published Balance Sheets as furnished to shareholders, and they are printed here (without any comment) by the kind permission of the respective Companies so that readers may see for themselves some forms adopted in practice.

	PAGE
AEOLIAN COMPANY LIMITED	112
ANGLO–DUTCH PLANTATIONS OF JAVA LIMITED..	118
BRITISH-AMERICAN TOBACCO COMPANY LIMITED	126
BRITISH DYESTUFFS CORPORATION LIMITED ..	130
COURTAULDS LIMITED	134
IMPERIAL TOBACCO COMPANY (OF GREAT BRITAIN AND IRELAND) LIMITED	136
LONDON AND SUBURBAN TRACTION COMPANY LIMITED	142
MEADOW DAIRY COMPANY LIMITED	148
UNDERGROUND ELECTRIC RAILWAYS COMPANY OF LONDON LIMITED	154
UNITED BRITISH OILFIELDS OF TRINIDAD LIMITED	168
VAN DEN BERGHS LIMITED	174
VICKERS LIMITED	180
AMERICAN COMPANIES—	
INTERNATIONAL HARVESTER COMPANY ..	185
INTERNATIONAL MERCANTILE MARINE COMPANY	190
IRON PRODUCTS CORPORATION	196
UNITED STATES STEEL CORPORATION ..	198

THE ÆOLIAN COM
Dr.   BALANCE SHEET

	£ s d	£ s d
To AUTHORISED CAPITAL :		
400,000 Ordinary Shares of £1 each	400,000 0 0	
*300,000 7½% Cumulative Preference Shares of £1 each	300,000 0 0	
	£700,000 0 0	
,, ISSUED CAPITAL :		
400,000 Ordinary Shares of £1 each	400,000 0 0	
250,000 7½% Cumulative Preference Shares of £1 each	250,000 0 0	
		650,000 0 0
,, MORTGAGE DEBENTURES :		
65 Debentures of £5,000 each issued as security for Bank Loan	325,000 0 0	
,, LOAN FROM BANKERS :		
Secured by deposit of Debentures as above		325,000 0 0
,, OTHER MORTGAGES ON FREEHOLD AND LEASEHOLD PROPERTIES		137,000 0 0
,, AEOLIAN CO., NEW YORK : Current Account		388,623 15 6
,, SUNDRY CREDITORS		87,393 1 2
,, BILLS PAYABLE		35,683 1 2
,, PREFERENCE DIVIDEND (*less* TAX) DUE 1ST JULY, 1922		6,796 17 6
,, RESERVE ACCOUNTS, VIZ. :		
Depreciation of Buildings, Plant and Machinery	131,179 5 11	
Hire Purchase Accounts and Library Subscriptions unexpired	20,350 0 0	
Balance of dividend from Subsidiary Company's Surplus Account	10,239 2 9	
		161,768 8 8
	Carried forward	1,792,265 4 0

PANY, LIMITED.
AT 30TH JUNE 1922.

Cr.

	£	s	d	£	s	d
By BOND STREET PROPERTY: As per valuation 28th July 1921				255,000	0	0
,, FREEHOLD PROPERTY AT HAYES AND SUNDERLAND, INCLUDING PLANT AND MACHINERY AT HAYES AT COST				389,591	13	10
,, FURNITURE AND FITTINGS, LONDON AND BRANCHES, *less* DEPRECIATION ..				27,763	14	9
,, INVESTMENTS IN CAPITAL STOCKS OF SUBSIDIARY COMPANIES				115,500	2	0
,, AMOUNTS DUE BY ALLIED AND SUBSIDIARY COMPANIES ON CURRENT ACCOUNT				110,909	11	8
,, INVESTMENT IN CAPITAL STOCK OF SUBSIDIARY COMPANY IN GERMANY AT COST	74,536	2	7			
Add : Balance due on Current Accounts	59,569	17	3			
	134,105	19	10			
Less : Reserve	96,633	13	8			
				37,472	6	2
,, TRADE INVESTMENTS AT COST				21,188	0	0
,, MORTGAGE REDEMPTION POLICY (Premiums Paid)				9,041	13	4
,, STOCKS OF MANUFACTURED GOODS, RAW MATERIAL, WORK IN PROGRESS, &c. As Certified by the Company's Officials				449,147	6	1
,, SUNDRY TRADE DEBTORS, *less* RESERVE FOR BAD AND DOUBTFUL ACCOUNTS				259,084	17	10
,, CLAIMS ADMITTED BY ANGLO-GERMAN MIXED TRIBUNAL				29,968	11	5
,, BILLS RECEIVABLE ..				41,137	18	10
Carried forward				1,745,805	15	11

The Aeolian Com

			Brought forward	1,792,265	4	0
To Profit & Loss Balance: As at 30th June 1921 ..	1,075	10	1			
Add : Balance from Profit and Loss Account ..	13,154	19	9			
	14,230	9	10			
Deduct : Preference Dividend for year less tax ..	13,359	7	6			
				871	2	4
				£1,793,136	6	4

* 7½% Cumulative Preference Shares guaranteed as to Principal and Pianola Company of New York.

The Company has guaranteed advances to a Subsidiary Company, &c.,
Signed on behalf of the Board of Directors as per resolution of

We report to the Shareholders that we have examined the above the information and explanations we have required. Subject to the opinion that such Balance Sheet is properly drawn up so as to exhibit a to the best of our information and the explanations given to us and as

3 Frederick's Place,
Old Jewry, London, E.C.2.
9th February 1923.

Dr.   PROFIT AND LOSS ACCOUNT

	£	s	d
To Loss on Trading for the Year after Providing for Depreciation (other than for Plant, Machinery, Furniture, Fittings, &c., covered by Reserve)	30,205	19	5
,, Debenture and Mortgage Interest	21,642	8	11
,, Balance Carried to Balance Sheet	13,154	19	9
	£65,003	8	1

pany, Limited.—(Contd.)

		£ s d
	Brought forward	1,745,805 15 11
By Cash at Bank and in Hand	.. .. ..	47,329 10 5
,, Trade Marks and Patents	.. .. ..	1 0 0
		£1,793,136 6 4

as to Interest up to 6% per annum by the Aeolian, Weber Piano and
up to £12,250.
meeting held 14th February 1923.

R. Williams-Bulkeley,
A. J. Mason, } *Directors.*

J. A. Findley, *Secretary.*

Balance Sheet with the books of the Company, and have obtained all book value of the investment in Germany (£37,472 6s. 2d.) we are of true and correct view of the state of the Company's affairs according shown by the Books of the company.

Price, Waterhouse & Co.

For the Year Ended 30th June 1922. *Cr.*

	£ s d	£ s d
By Dividends from Investments in Subsidiary Companies (Accumulated Surplus), and Other Companies	72,729 8 11	
Less : Appropriated to Reserves	57,500 12 3	
		15,228 16 8
,, Part Proceeds of Claims Received or Admitted by Anglo-German Tribunal		49,774 11 5
		£65,003 8 1

The Aeolian Com

AMALGAMATED

of the Assets and Liabilities at 30th June 1922 of The Aeolian

(Note.—The Book Value of the investments in Germany is shown

Dr.

	£ s d	£ s d
To Issued Capital of the Aeolian Co. Ltd.: 400,000 Ordinary Shares of £1 each	400,000 0 0	
*250,000 7½% Cumulative Preference Shares of £1 each	250,000 0 0	
		650,000 0 0
,, Mortgage Debentures: 65 Debentures of £5,000 each issued as security for Bank Loan	325,000 0 0	
,, Loan from Bankers: Secured by Deposit of Debentures as above		325,000 0 0
,, Other Mortgages on Freehold and Leasehold Properties		137,000 0 0
,, Aeolian Company, New York, Current Account		388,623 15 6
,, Sundry Creditors		112,871 3 2
,, Bills Payable		39,525 9 11
,, Preference Dividend (less Tax) Due 1st July 1922		6,796 17 6
,, Reserve Accounts, viz.: Depreciation of Buildings, Plant and Machinery, &c	149,665 4 5	
Hire Purchase Accounts and Library Subscriptions unexpired	22,625 15 9	
Balance of Capital Surplus Accounts	27,766 16 7	
		200,057 16 9
,. Profit and Loss Account Balance		5,000 12 11
One of the companies is contingently liable under guarantee up to £2,250.		
		£1,864,875 15 9

* 7½% Cumulative Preference Shares guaranteed as to Principal and and Pianola Company. of New York.

pany, Limited.—(Contd.)
STATEMENT

Co., Ltd., and of the Companies of which it is sole proprietor.
separately and has not been allocated to the various headings.)

	£	s	d	Cr. £	s	d
By Bond Street Property: As per Valuation, 28th July 1921				255,000	0	0
,, Freehold Property Including Plant and Machinery at Cost				468,980	6	4
,, Furniture and Fittings *Less* Depreciation				35,956	5	9
,, Investments in Capital Stocks of Subsidiary Companies in Germany at Cost	134,009	15	5			
Add: Balance due on Current Accounts	59,569	17	3			
	193,579	12	8			
Less: Reserve	138,579	12	8			
				55,000	0	0
,, Amounts due by Allied Companies on Current Account				6,654	4	1
,, Trade Investments at Cost				42,032	10	10
,, Mortgage Redemption Policy 1 remiums Paid				9,041	13	4
,, Stocks of Manufactured Goods, Raw Materials, Work in Progress, &c., As certified by the Company's Officials				516,520	5	11
,, Sundry Debtors, *less* Reserves for Bad and Doubtful Debts				354,012	9	5
,, Claims Admitted by Anglo-German Mixed Tribunal				29,968	11	5
,, Bills Receivable				42,149	18	10
,, Cash at Bank and in Hand				49,556	9	10
,, Trade Marks & Patents				3	0	0
				£1,864,875	15	9

as to Interest up to 6% per annum by the Aeolian, Weber Piano

THE ANGLO-DUTCH PLAN

(The Company owning the entire issued Capital of the Maatschappij which are, for the information of the Share

Dr.   BALANCE SHEET,

	£ s d	£ s d
To CAPITAL: Authorised and Registered— 2,250,000 Shares of £1 each	2,250,000 0 0	
Issued and Subscribed— 1,930,170 Shares of £1 each		1,930,170 0 0
,, CAPITAL RESERVE ACCT.: Bonus declared by the Pamanoekan en Tjiassemlanden Maatschappij in 1919, in respect of Expropriation .. .. .. 1,376,012 4 1 *Less:* Underwriting Commission, &c., written off in 1919 £64,838 9 0 643,390 Bonus Shares allotted as fully paid, in accordance with Resolution of the 19th November, 1920 .. .. 643,390 0 0	708,228 9 0	
	667,783 15 1	
Exchange Differences— Differences in Exchange on remittances of £1,514,223 7s. 6d. in 1919 and 1920 .. 138,211 3 5 *Less:* Difference in Exchange on remittances to Java in 1920 .. 13,762 19 0	124,448 4 5	
		792,231 19 6
,, SUNDRY CREDITORS AND CREDIT BALANCES ..		85,681 14 6
,, UNCLAIMED DIVIDENDS..		5,483 1 1
	Carried forward	2,813,566 15 1

TATIONS OF JAVA, LTD.

ter Exploitatie der Pamanoekan en Tjiassemlanden, the Accounts of holders, presented on the following pages.)

31ST DECEMBER 1920.   *Cr.*

	£	s	d	£	s	d
By Cost of 2,700 "B" Shares and 2,500 "C" Shares of F.1000 each in the Maatsschappij ter Exploitatie der Pamanoekan en Tjiassemlanden, and Amount Advanced for the Redemption of F.2,079,000 4% Deb. Bonds of that Company—per last Account				706,485	18	11
,, Maatschappij ter Exploitatie der Pamanoekan en Tjiassemlanden for Advances and Interest thereon ..	946,817	4	5			
Add : Amount declared as Dividend for 1920	21,607	15	0			
				968,424	19	5
,, Sundry Debtors and Debit Balances ..				11,212	0	2
,, Investments in Government Securities at Cost :— £92,000 Exchequer Bonds, 1922 £160,000 ,, ,, 1921 £500,000 National War Bonds, 1922 £390,000 ,, ,, 1923 £50,000 ,, ,, 1925 £131,600 ,, ,, 1927 £25,000 War Loan 5%, 1929-47				1,303,991	2	8

(Note.—The value of these Investments at middle market price on the date of the Balance Sheet was £1,306,375.)

By Payment on Account of the purchase of Shares in the Sumatra Land Syndicate, Ltd.				10,000	0	0
			Carried forward	3,000,114	1	2

H

The Anglo-Dutch Planta

	£ s d	£ s d
Brought forward		2,813,566 15 1
To REVENUE ACCOUNT:		
Balance per last Account	273,661 2 0	
Less: Dividends paid 14th May and 19th November 1920	225,186 10 0	
	48,474 12 0	
Add: Balance per subjoined Account	147,186 10 8	
		195,661 2 8
		£3,009,227 17 9

C. H. STRUTT,
W. H. DAUKES,
    Directors.
FRANCIS PEEK & CO., LIMITED, *Secretaries.*

REPORT OF THE AUDITORS TO THE SHAREHOLDERS OF

We have examined the accounts of the Company and have obtained opinion the above Balance Sheet is properly drawn up so as to exhibit to the best of our information and the explanations given to us, and as
5 London Wall Buildings, E.C.
21*st October* 1921.

REVENUE ACCOUNT FOR THE

	£ s d	£ s d
To DIRECTORS' REMUNERATION		
Fixed	2,250 0 0	
Additional in accordance with Article 86	7,359 6 7	
		9,609 6 7
,, Managing Director's Salary		1,000 0 0
,, General Expenses, including Rent, Secretarial and Clerical, *less* Transfer Fees		5,719 2 10
,, Stamp Duty and Expenses in connection with increase of Capital and Distribution of Bonus Shares		8,529 17 4
,, Reserve for Corporation Profits Tax		6,000 0 0
,, Balance—Profit for 1920		147,186 10 8
		£178,044 17 5

tions of Java, Ltd.— *(Contd.)*

	Brought forward	3,000,114	1 2
By CASH AT BANKERS, London and Amsterdam, and in hand		9113	16 7

£3,009,227 17 9

THE ANGLO-DUTCH PLANTATIONS OF JAVA, LIMITED.

all the information and explanations we have required. In our a true and correct view of the state of the Company's affairs, according shown by the books of the Company.

DELOITTE, PLENDER, GRIFFITHS & CO.,
Chartered Accountants,
Auditors.

YEAR ENDED 31ST DECEMBER 1920.

	£ s d
By Amount declared as dividend for the year 1920 on the Share Capital of the Maatschappij ter Exploitatie der Pamanoekan en Tjiassemlanden, and Interest on Advances to that Company	93,134 15 11
,, Dividends and Interest received and accrued on Investments, &c.	84,226 4 5
,, Bank Interest, &c.	683 17 1

£178,044 17 5

The Anglo-Dutch Planta

RECOMMENDED APPRO

	£	s	d
Interim Dividend 5%, paid 18th April 1921	72,381	7	6
Payment of a Final Dividend of 5%	72,381	7	6
Balance carried forward	50,898	7	8
	£195,661	2	8

MAATSCHAPPIJ TER EXPLOITATIE DER

(The entire issued Capital of this Company is owned

BALANCE SHEET

(Exchange has been

LIABILITIES.

	F.	F.	£	s	d
To CAPITAL— Authorised .. 7,500,000.00					
Issued		5,200,000.00	433,333	6	8
,, ANGLO-DUTCH PLANTATIONS OF JAVA, LTD.—					
Current Ac... 11,361,806.62					
Debenture Redemption Account .. 2,079,000.00		13,440,806.62	1,120,067	4	5
,, RESERVE ACCOUNTS—					
Reserve for Depreciation on Buildings and Machinery .. 1,072,571.22					
Reserve for Cinchona Uprootings 172,300.00					
Reserve for Teak Exploitation 491,619.84		1,736,491.06	144,707	11	9
,, SUNDRY CREDITORS		1,483,596.04	123,633	0	1
Carried forward		21,860,893.72	1,821,741	2	11

tions of Java, Ltd.—(Contd.)

PRIATION OF REVENUE.

	£	s	d
Balance from last Account (after deduction of dividends paid 14th May and 19th November 1920)	48,474	12	0
Balance of Revenue Account for the year 1920 ..	147,186	10	8
	£195,661	2	8

PAMANOEKAN EN TJIASSEMLANDEN.

by the Anglo-Dutch Plantations of Java, Ltd.)

31ST DECEMBER 1920.

taken at F.12 to the £.)

ASSETS.

	F.	£	s	d
BY FREEHOLD PROPERTIES, comprising areas under cultivation of Tea, Cinchona, Coffee and Rubber; Teak Forests and Undeveloped Lands; Factories, Buildings, Machinery, Plant; Roads, Bridges, Forest Railways, and Electric Power Station	15,768,024.23	1,314,002	0	5
(NOTE.—In view of the opinion of the Board that the value of the above-mentioned Assets remaining after the expropriation by the Netherlands Indies Government during 1919, of certain Ownership Rights and Properties exceeded the book figure of cost, nothing was written off in respect of such expropriation.)				
Add : Expenditure in 1920	3,808,003.64	317,333	12	8
	19,576,027.87	1,631,335	13	1
Carried forward	19,576,027.87	1,631,335	13	1

Maatschappij ter Exploitatie der

	Brought forward	21,860,893.72	1,821,741	2	11
To BANK OVERDRAFT		373,913.91	31,159	9	10
,, PROFIT & LOSS ACCOUNT— Profit for the Year 1920 per subjoined Accounts [subject to War Taxes (Java) if any]		259,293.02	21,607	15	0
		F.22,494,100.65	£1,874,508	7	9

TO THE SHAREHOLDERS OF THE MAATSCHAPPIJ TER
We have examined the above Balance Sheet with the books and Monthly Cash Accounts signed by the Managers of the Departments, Balance Sheet is properly drawn up so as to exhibit a true and correct information and the explanations given to us, and as shown by the books

Soebang,
Java, *9th August* 1921.

Dr.   PROFIT AND LOSS ACCOUNT FOR

	F.	£	s	d
To SUPERANNUATION ALLOWANCES	26,624.65	2,218	14	5
,, DEPRECIATION OF BUILDINGS AND MACHINERY ..	152,909.44	12,742	9	1
,, CATCH-CROPS, &c., uprooted	77,424.39	6.452	0	8
,, INTEREST ON ADVANCES by the Anglo-Dutch Plantations of Java, Ltd. ..	858,324.56	71,527	0	11
,, PROFIT FOR THE YEAR ended 31st December 1920 ..	259,293.02	21,607	15	0
	F. 1,374,576.06	£114,548	0	1

Pamanoekan en Tjiassemlanden. (Contd.)

	Brought forward	19,576,027.87	1,631,335	13	1
By STOCKS—					
Tea, Coffee and Rubber (at Sale or Market price) ..		972,512.19	81,042	13	8
Cinchona (at Sale or Contract price)		351,442.58	29,286	17	8
Rice, Paddy and Dedek (at Sale or Contract price)		593,678.28	49,473	3	9
Teak Sleepers, Sawn Timber, &c. (at Sale or Market Price)		190,209.00	15,850	15	0
Stores, Materials, Chests, &c. (at Cost Price) ..		308,304.08	25,692	0	2
,, SUNDRY DEBTORS		319,403.28	26,616	18	9
,, CASH AT BANKERS AND IN HAND		182,523.37	15,210	5	8
		F.22,494,100.65	£1,874,508	7	9

EXPLOITATIE DER PAMANOEKAN EN TJIASSEMLANDEN.
other documents relating thereto, in which have been incorporated the
the books of which have been audited by us. In our opinion the above
view of the state of the Company's affairs, according to the best of our
of the Company.

    p.p. FRANCIS PEEK & COMPANY, LIMITED.
      WILLIAM BIRNIE, } *Chartered Accountants.*
      C. H. BIRTWHISTLE, }

THE YEAR ENDED 31ST DECEMBER 1920.   Cr.

BY PROFITS FROM DEPARTMENTS :—

	F.	£ s d	F.	£	s	d
Tea ..			419,134.80	34,927	18	0
Quinine			437,041.65	36,420	2	9
Rubber Profit	1,192,663.58	99,388 12 7				
Less : Coffee Loss	27,262.95	2,271 18 3				
			1,165,400.63	97,116	14	4
Rice and Rice Mill			90,120.64	7,510	1	1
Wood..			299,472.10	24,956	0	2
			2,411,169.82	200,930	16	4
Less : Administration and General Expenses attributable to Revenue Account in respect of Salaries of Representative and Staff, Verponding and Income Tax, Medical Service and Interest, including Agency, Accountancy and Audit, and Batavia Office Charges			1,036,593.76	86,382	16	3
			F.1,374,576.06	£114,548	0	1

BRITISH-AMERICAN TOBAC

Dr. PROFIT AND LOSS ACCOUNT FOR

	£	s	d	£	s	d
To DIVIDENDS PAID :						
Preference	225,000	0	0			
Ordinary—four interim Dividends	2,566,555	11	2			
				2,791,555	11	2
,, BALANCE CARRIED TO BALANCE SHEET				1,609,228	3	4
				£4,400,783	14	6

Dr. BALANCE SHEET,

	£	s	d	£	s	d
To CAPITAL AUTHORISED :						
4,500,000 Five per cent. Cumulative Preference Shares of £1 each	4,500,000	0	0			
18,000,000 Ordinary Shares of £1 each	18,000,000	0	0			
	£22,500,000	0	0			
,, CAPITAL ISSUED :						
4,500,000 Five per cent. Cumulative Preference Shares of £1 each	4,500,000	0	0			
16,046,070 Ordinary Shares of £1 each	16,046,070	0	0			
				20,546,070	0	0
,, CREDITORS AND CREDIT BALANCES				5,161,821	13	8
,, RESERVES FOR BUILDINGS, MACHINERY AND MATERIALS				500,000	0	0
,, PREMIUM ON ORDINARY SHARES ISSUED..				417,314	0	0
,, PROVISION FOR REDEMPTION OF COUPONS				48,445	16	9
,, SPECIAL RESERVE				1,256,398	12	2
,, PROFIT AND LOSS ACCOUNT						
Balance brought forward from previous year	3,171,454	2	9			
Less, Final Dividend of Eight per cent. for the year ended 30th September 1921	1,281,266	6	5			
Carried forward	1,890,187	16	4	27,930,050	2	7

CO COMPANY, LIMITED.
THE YEAR ENDED 30TH SEPTEMBER 1922. *Cr.*

	£ s d
By DIRECT PROFITS AND DIVIDENDS for the year after deducting all charges and expenses for management, &c., and providing for Income Tax and Corporation Profits Tax ..	4,400,783 14 6
	£4,400,783 14 6

30TH SEPTEMBER 1922. *Cr.*

	£ s d
By REAL ESTATE AND BUILDINGS AT COST, less provision for amortisation of Leaseholds ..	490,558 6 9
,, PLANT, MACHINERY, FURNITURE AND FITTINGS AT COST OR UNDER	529,246 16 2
,, GOODWILL, TRADE MARKS AND PATENTS ..	200,000 0 0
,, LOANS TO AND CURRENT ACCOUNTS WITH ASSOCIATED COMPANIES	4,695,581 13 8
,, INVESTMENTS IN ASSOCIATED COMPANIES ..	15,266,302 2 11
,, BRITISH GOVERNMENT SECURITIES	464,853 15 0
,, STOCKS OF LEAF, Manufactured Goods and Materials at Cost or under	4,849,512 19 9
,, SUNDRY DEBTORS (*less* provision for Doubtful Debts) AND DEBIT BALANCES	1,659,489 4 10
,, CASH AT BANKERS, in Transit and at Call ..	4,495,610 17 2
Carried forward	32,651,155 16 3

British-American Tobacco

Brought forward	1,890,187	16	4	27,930,050	2	7
Less Amount appropriated and applied in making payment in full for 310 Ordinary Shares at £1 per Share, in accordance with Extraordinary Resolution of 10th May, 1920, and distributed to the Ordinary Shareholders at the rate of 1 Share for every 4 Shares held	310	0	0			
	1,889,877	16	4			
Add Portion of the General Reserve of £1,500,000 set up in 1914 to provide against possible losses arising from the War not now required ..	1,221,999	14	0			
Balance—Year to 30th September 1922 as above	1,609,228	3	4			
				4,721,105	13	8
				£32,651,155	16	3

There are Contingent Liabilities as follows :
 (1) On Shares not fully paid, £25,465 19s. 3d.
 (2) For premiums payable on Redemption of Shares in Associated Companies allocated to Employees.
 (3) In respect of Guarantees given on behalf of certain Associated Companies.
 (4) To issue 837 Ordinary Shares of £1 each in accordance with the Extraordinary Resolution of 10th May 1920 to Shareholders who have not lodged acceptances.

To the Shareholders of the British-

I have examined the above Balance Sheet with the books of the Branches and Depots certified by the respective Managers, and I have
In my opinion the Balance Sheet is properly drawn up so as to exhibit to the best of the information and the explanations given me. and as various Branches and Depots.

5 London Wall Buildings,
 Finsbury Circus, E.C.2.
  20*th December* 1922.

Company, Limited.—*(Contd.)*

Brought forward   32,651,155   16   3

£32,651,155   16   3

Approved on behalf of the Board,
      A. G. JEFFRESS,
      S. J. GILLCHREST,
           Directors.

    A. M. RICKARDS, *Secretary*.

AMERICAN TOBACCO CO., LTD.

Company in London, in which are incorporated the Returns from the obtained all the information and explanations I have required.
a true and correct view of the state of the Company's affairs according shown by the books of the Company, and the Returns received from the

        WM. PLENDER,
          Auditor
    (DELOITTE, PLENDER, GRIFFITHS & CO.),
       Chartered Accountants.

BRITISH DYESTUFFS
BALANCE SHEET,

CAPITAL AND LIABILITIES.	£	s	d	£	s	d
SHARE CAPITAL:						
AUTHORISED.						
£10,000,000, divided into 4,500,000 Pref. Shares, 4,500,000 Preferred Ord. Shares, and 1,000,000 Def. Ord. Shares, all of £1 each						
ISSUED.						
Preference Shares—						
4,116,404 Shares fully paid	4,116,404	0	0			
Preferred Ord. Shares—						
4,085,081 Shares, fully paid	4,085,081	0	0			
Deferred Ord. Shares—						
993,505 Shares, fully paid	993,505	0	0			
				9,194,990	0	0
SUNDRY CREDITORS (including Bills Payable)				481,753	16	7
RESERVE FOR RESEARCH ..				100,000	0	0

£9,776,743 16 7

AUDITORS' REPORT TO
We beg to report to the Shareholders of British Dyestuffs Corpora
Company, and that we have obtained all the information and explana
In our opinion the foregoing Balance Sheet is properly drawn up so as
according to the best of our information and the explanations given to

CORPORATION, LIMITED.
31st October 1921.

	ASSETS. £	s	d	£	s	d
Shares Acquired in Associated Companies (after making provision for losses included in the £1,006,660 2s. 10d. undermentioned)..	1,451,044	7	2			
Advances to Associated Companies ..	6,539,817	0	3			
				*7,990,861	7	5
Cash at Bank, on Hand and Treasury Bills ..				188,829	9	4
Freehold Offices and Equipment ..				63,183	15	1
Sundry Debtors ..				471,040	6	7
Bills Receivable ..				7,921	11	11
Preliminary Expenses ..				251,551	16	0
Profit and Loss Account:						
Loss for year ..	1,006,660	2	10			
Deduct Balance at 31st October 1920 ..	203,304	12	7			
				803,355	10	3

William Alexander,
Henry Birchenough,
Directors.

Manchester,
9th June 1922.

£9,776,743 16 7

* A summary of the Assets and Liabilities of Associated Companies is enclosed.

THE SHAREHOLDERS.

tion, Limited, that we have audited the Books and Accounts of the tions required by us.
to exhibit a true and correct view of the state of the Company's affairs, us, and as shown by the books of the Company.

Thomson McLintock & Co.

Bond Court House, Walbrook, London.
13th June 1922.

British Dyestuffs Corporation, Limited.—(*Contd.*)

ACCOUNTS FOR YEAR ENDED 31ST OCTOBER 1921.

The following is a Summary of the combined Assets and Liabilities of Associated Companies:—

ASSETS.	£	s	d
Land, Buildings, Plant and Machinery, as per last account	4,318,702	19	5
Additions during year	230,712	0	5
	4,549,414	19	10
Less Provision for Depreciation during year	461,209	16	0
	4,088,205	3	10
Stocks (at cost or market price whichever is lower)	2,507,135	19	2
Sundry Debtors and Investments (including claims for refund of Excess Profits Duty)	930,737	17	2
Cash on hand	1,492	5	1
	7,527,571	5	3

LIABILITIES.			
Sundry Creditors (excluding Advances made by British Dyestuffs Corporation, Limited)	525,564	2	4
	7,002,007	2	11
Value of Goodwill, Patents and other Rights satisfied in terms of Agreement by an issue of Deferred Ordinary Shares	1,000,000	0	0
	8,002,007	2	11
Less Merger value of Shares in subsidiary Companies held by shareholders who have not exchanged their holdings	11,145	15	6
	£7,990,861	7	5

9th June 1922.

Dr.   COURTAULDS,
BALANCE SHEET,

	£	s	d	£	s	d
To Share Capital: Authorised and Issued: 12,000,000 Shares of £1 each, fully paid				12,000,000	0	0
,, Creditors and Special Reserves in Respect of Taxation (including Debenture Stocks £8,125)				3,599,192	2	1
,, General Reserve Account				2,000,000	0	0
,, Profit and Loss Account Balance for the year 1922: After crediting, as usual, Interest and Dividends on the Viscose Company Shares, and all other Investments, and after writing off £300,000 and providing a further £250,000, to meet the present and any further fall in values of Buildings and Plant	3,018,431	18	3			
Add Balance from last year £1,168,466 19 9						
Less Final Dividend for 1921, paid 13th March 1922, free of tax 750,000 0 0						
	418,466	19	9			
	3,436,898	18	0			
Deduct— Interim Dividend for 1922, paid 3rd August 1922, free of tax 750,000 0 0 General Reserve Account 1,000,000 0 0						
	1,750,000	0	0			
				1,686,898	18	0
				£19,286,091	0	1

Report of the Auditors to the Share

We have audited the Balance Sheet of your Company, dated 31st mation and explanations we have required.

In our opinion such Balance Sheet is properly drawn up so as to according to the best of our information and the explanations given

21st *February* 1923.

LIMITED.
31ST DECEMBER 1922.

Cr.

	£	s	d	£	s	d
By FREEHOLD AND LEASEHOLD PROPERTY, PLANT, MACHINERY AND FIXTURES				1,655,873	11	7
,, STOCK-IN-TRADE AND SUNDRY STORES				1,158,745	12	3
,, INVESTMENTS :						
British Government Securities and other Investments	6,909,802	11	7			
Shares in the American Viscose Corporation	7,804,021	6	9			
				14,713,823	18	4

All the above Investments, except additions made during the year, are taken at the valuation included in last year's Balance Sheet, or at market prices if less than such valuation ; the additions are taken at cost, or at market prices if less than cost.

The value taken for the Shares in the American Viscose Corporation received in exchange for Shares in the Viscose Company is the same as that put upon the latter in November 1920.

	£	s	d
,, DEBTORS (less RESERVE), INCLUDING BILLS RECEIVABLE AND PAYMENTS IN ADVANCE	555,484	9	8
,, CASH AT BANKERS AND IN HAND	1,202,163	8	3
	£19,286,091	0	1

SAMUEL COURTAULD,
T. P. LATHAM,
            Directors.

HOLDERS OF MESSRS. COURTAULDS, LIMITED.
December 1922, as above set forth, and have obtained all the infor-

exhibit a true and correct view of the state of the Company's affairs, to us and as shown by the books of the Company.

W. ELLES-HILL & CO.,
PRICE, WATERHOUSE & CO., } *Joint Auditors.*
        Chartered Accountants.

THE IMPERIAL TOBACCO COMPANY (OF
Dr.   BALANCE SHEET,

	£	s	d	£	s	d
To CAPITAL AUTHORISED :						
6,000,000 " A " 5½ per cent. Cumulative Preference Shares ..	6,000,000	0	0			
6,000,000 " B " 6 per cent. Non-Cumulative Preference Shares ..	6,000,000	0	0			
3,000,000 " C " 10 per cent. Non-Cumulative Preference Shares ..	3,000,000	0	0			
30,000,000 Ordinary Shares ..	30,000,000	0	0			
	£45,000,000	0	0			
,, CAPITAL ISSUED :						
4,959,249 " A " 5½ per cent. Cumulative Preference Shares ..				4,959,249	0	0
5,260,469 " B " 6 per cent. Non-Cumulative Preference Shares ..				5,260,469	0	0
2,638,218 " C " 10 per cent. Non-Cumulative Preference Shares ..				2,638,218	0	0
22,472,658 Ordinary Shares..				22,472,658	0	0
				35,330,594	0	0
,, CREDITORS, including provision for Taxation, Bonus to Customers, estimated Capital Liability under Dividend Guarantees, Employers' Liability, Marine and other Funds				11,142,585	15	7
,, PROVISION FOR PENSIONS, &c.				1,610,362	4	10
,, PREMIUM ON ISSUE OF ORDINARY SHARES ..	5,595,446	0	0			
,, GENERAL RESERVE ACCT : per last Balance Sheet .. 6,178,877 0 0 Add: Transfer from Profit and Loss Account .. 225,677 0 0	6,404,554	0	0			
				12,000,000	0	0
			Carried forward	60,083,542	0	5

GREAT BRITAIN AND IRELAND), LIMITED.
31st October 1922.   *Cr.*

	£	s	d
By Land, Buildings, Plant and Machinery—at cost, less amounts written off	4,166,748	11	4
„ Goodwill and Patent Rights	9,422,581	16	0
„ Investments in Associated Companies—at cost, or below in those cases where depreciation has taken place, and Current Accounts with Associated Companies	6,017,612	6	11
Note.—In the aggregate the market value of these investments is largely in excess of the book value.			
„ Stock-in-Trade—at or under cost, less amounts set aside to meet fluctuations in the value of leaf tobacco	31,998,859	0	8
„ Payments on Account of Leaf in Transit, &c.	1,246,673	0	9
„ Debtors, *less* Reserve for Discounts and doubtful Debts	5,860,413	2	0
„ Bills Receivable	319	7	8
„ Investments in Government Stocks, County Council and Corporation Stocks, Railway Debenture and Preference Stocks—valued at ruling prices at date	1,019,416	11	7
„ Cash at Bankers and in Hand	4,716,365	6	0
Carried forward	64,448,989	2	11

The Imperial Tobacco Company (of

			Brought forward	60,083,542	0	5
To Profit and Loss Account:						
Balance for the year	6,273,399 18 3					
Balance at 31st October 1921, after deducting Customers' Bonus to that date	203,600 17 8					
	6,477,000 15 11					
Deduct: Interim Dividends paid :						
on "A" 5½ per cent. Cumulative Preference Shares	136,379 7 0					
on "B" 6 per cent. Non-Cumulative Preference Shares	157,814 1 5					
on "C" 10 per cent. Non-Cumulative Preference Shares	131,910 18 0					
on Ordinary Shares	1,685,449 7 0					
		2,111,553 13 5				
				4,365,447	2	6
				£64,448,989	2	11

Memo.—(*a*) There are Contingent Liabilities of the nature of Guarantees of Dividends on Shares in two Associated Companies.
(*b*) There is an uncalled Liability on Investments held of £142,791 15s. 0d.

Auditor's Report to the Shareholders of the Imperial

I have examined the above Balance Sheet dated 31st October 1922, porated the Audited Accounts of the Branches, and have obtained such Balance Sheet is properly drawn up so as to exhibit a true and of my information and the explanations given me, and as shown by

5 London Wall Buildings, E.C.2.
23rd *January* 1923.

Great Britain and Ireland) Ltd.—(*Contd.*)

Brought forward 64,448,989 2 11

£64,448,989 2 11

REGINALD MONCKTON,   GEO. A. WILLS, *Chairman.*
(Chartered Accountant),   H. W. GUNN, *Deputy-Chairman.*
Chief Accountant.   GEORGE A. FALK, *Secretary.*

TOBACCO COMPANY (OF GREAT BRITAIN AND IRELAND), LIMITED.
with the books at the Head Office in Bristol, in which have been incor-
all the information and explanations I have required. In my opinion
correct view of the state of the Company's affairs according to the best
the books of the Company.

WM. PLENDER,
Auditor
(Deloitte, Plender, Griffiths & Co.),
Chartered Accountant.

The Imperial Tobacco Company (of

Dr.   PROFIT AND LOSS ACCOUNT

	£	s	d
To Provision for Pensions	200,000	0	0
„ Amount written off Freehold Buildings, in addition to normal Depreciation	500,000	0	0
„ Transfer to General Reserve Account	225,677	0	0
„ Balance carried to Balance Sheet	6,273,399	18	3
	£7,199,076	18	3

Dr.   APPROPRIATION

	£	s	d	£	s	d
To Dividends on " A " 5½ per cent. Cumulative Preference Shares—						
Interim Dividend to 30th April 1922, paid 1st July 1922	136,379	7	0			
Final Dividend to 31st October 1922, payable 1st Jan. 1923	136,379	7	0			
				272,758	14	0
„ Dividends on " B " 6 per cent. Non-Cumulative Preference Shares :						
Interim Dividend to 30th April 1922, paid 1st August 1922	157,814	1	5			
Final Dividend to 31st October 1922, payable 1st Feb 1923	157,814	1	5			
				315,628	2	10
„ Dividends on " C " 10 per cent. Non-Cumulative Pref. Shares—						
Interim Dividend to 30th April 1922, paid 1st August 1922	131,910	18	0			
Final Dividend to 31st October 1922, payable 1st Feb. 1923	131,910	18	0			
				263,821	16	0
„ Dividends on Ordinary Shares— Interim Dividend of 7½ per cent. paid 1st September 1922 (free of income-tax)	1,685,449	7	0			
Proposed Final Dividend of 7½ per cent. (free of income-tax)	1,685,449	7	0			
Proposed Bonus of 1s. 6d. per share (free of income-tax)	1,685,449	7	0			
				5,056,348	1	0
„ Balance carried forward				568,444	2	1
				£6,477,000	15	11

Great Britain and Ireland) Ltd.—(*Contd.*)
FOR THE YEAR ENDED 31ST OCTOBER 1922.   *Cr.*

	£	s	d
By Net Trading Profit and Interest and Dividends on Investments (including Dividends from Companies operating outside the United Kingdom), and Loans, after providing for Director ' Fees and Management Remuneration, Depreciation of Freehold Buildings, Plant and Machinery, Sundry Reserves (including provision for Taxation), Working ing Expenses, Head Office and Registration Charges, and Bonus to Customers	7,194,556	13	3
,, Transfer and other Fees	4,520	5	0
	£7,199,076	18	3

ACCOUNT.   *Cr.*

	£	s	d
By Balance from Profit and Loss Account for the year	6,273,399	18	3
,, Balance of undivided Profit at 31st October 1921, after deducting Customer's Bonus to that date	203,600	17	8

£5,477,000 15 11

THE LONDON AND SUBURBAN
Dr. BALANCE SHEET,

Year 1921

	£ s d	£ s d	£
To SHARE CAPITAL: AUTHORISED			
1,700,000 5 per cent. Cumulative Preference Shares of £1 each	1,700,000 0 0		
1,900,000 Ordinary Shares of £1 each	1,900,000 0 0		
	£3,600,000 0 0		
ISSUED			
5 per cent. Cumulative Preference Shares (including fractional coupons outstanding)	1,603,456 8 0		
Ordinary Shares (including fractional coupons outstanding)	1,846,104 10 0		
		3,449,560 18 0	3,449,561
To LOAN CAPITAL: AUTHORISED			
An amount equal to one-half of the Share Capital issued and outstanding.			
ISSUED			
4½ per cent. First Mortgage Debenture Stock (including fractional coupons outstanding)—Part of an issue limited by the Trust Deed to £550,000	532,634 16 0		
Less Amount issued to the Trustees of the 5 per cent. "A" Debenture Stock as security	350,000 0 0		
		182,634 16 0	182,635
5 per cent. "A" Debenture Stock	350,000 0 0		
Less Amount Purchased and Cancelled	118,287 0 0		
		231,713 0 0	254,913
,, ASSOCIATED COMPANIES— DEPOSITS		62,650 0 0	116,200
,, SUNDRY CREDITORS AND CREDIT BALANCES		16,177 19 2	17,758
,, INTEREST ON THE 4½ PER CENT. DEB. STOCK, payable 1st Jan. 1923, less tax		3,081 14 6	2,876
	Carried forward	3,945,818 7 8	4,023,943

TRACTION COMPANY, LIMITED.
31ST DECEMBER 1922.

Cr.

Year 1921

	£	s	d	£	s	d	£

BY SHARES HELD IN OTHER COMPANIES, at cost, viz.:

   MET. ELECTRIC TRAMWAYS, LIMITED.
   456,667 5% Cum. Pref. Shares of £1 each, fully paid .. ..
   463,951 Ord. Shares of £1 each, fully paid ..

   LONDON UNITED TRAMWAYS LIMITED.
   116,443 5% Pref. Shares of £1 each, fully paid
   2,228,295 Ord. Shares of 5s. each, fully paid

   TRAMWAYS (M.E.T.) OMNIBUS CO., LIMITED.
   200,000 Ord. Shares of £1 each, 1s. paid ..

   SOUTH MET. ELECTRIC TRAMS & LIGHTING CO., LTD.
   168,246 6% Cum. Pref. Shares of £1 each, fully paid .. ..
   181,190 Ord. Shares of £1 each, fully paid ..

                                                                              3,733,884 10 7   3,736,458

NOTE.—Under a scheme of arrangement the Capital of the London United Tramways, Ltd., was reduced in 1919 and 70,693 Preference Shares and 2,228,295 Ordinary Shares are now held in the place of the 68 Third Debs. of £1,000 each, 121,820 5% Cum. Pref. Shares of £10 each and 97,987 Ordinary Shares of £10 each originally held.

All the holdings of the Company set out above remain in the books at the original cost.

                       Carried forward   3,733,884 10 7   3,736,458

The London and Suburban

		Brought forward	3,945,818	7	8	4,023,943
To Interest on the 5 per cent. " A " Debenture Stock accrued to date, *less* tax			1,810	5	6	1,859
,, 5 per cent. " A " Debenture Stock Service Fund—						
As per last Account		75,601 10 4				
Add further provision in 1922 as per Revenue Account		17,936 7 0				
Interest on Deposit		1 13 6				
			93,539	10	10	75,602
,, Revenue Account :						
Dividend on 5 per cent. Cumulative Freference Shares—						
Balance of 4 per cent. in respect of the year 1918		64,138 4 10				
1 per cent. on account of the year 1919		16,034 11 2				
		80,172 16 0				56,121
Amount carried forward		17,243 7 7				11,523
			97,416	3	7	

£4,138,584 7 7   £4,169,048

Arrears of Preference Dividend
 to date, £304,656 14s. 4d.

Auditors'

We have examined the above Balance Sheet, dated 31st December 1922,
information and explanations we have required. We are of opinion that,
made by the subsidiary Companies, such Balance Sheet is properly drawn
affairs, according to the best of our information and the explanations given
 London, E.C.
  23rd *February* 1923.

Traction Company, Ltd.—(Contd.)

Brought forward				3,733,884	10	7	3,736,458	
By PRELIMINARY EXPENDITURE, as per last account (*less* Credit)	14,992	16	7					
Loss on realisation of Shares of the Gearless Motor Omnibus Co., Ltd.	4,581	6	3					
				19,574	2	10	15,013	
,, DISCOUNT ON ISSUE OF 5% " A " DEB. STOCK, as per last Account	24,895	2	5					
Less discount on Deb. Stock purchased and cancelled	3,596	17	0					
				21,298	5	5	24,895	
,, SUNDRY DEBTORS AND DEBIT BALANCES :								
Met. Electric Tramways, Ltd.—Loan, secured by lien on Shares of the North Met. Electric Power Supply Co.	70,000	0	0					
Associated Companies for dividends (*less* tax)	85,726	1	6					
Other Accounts ..	36,755	0	3					
				192,481	1	9	206,620	
,, £52,150 2s. 7d. 3½% War Stock, 1925-28, at cost ..				50,000	0	0		
,, CASH ON DEPOSIT AND CURRENT ACCOUNT—5% " A " Debenture Stock Service Fund				2,003	14	2		
,, CASH ON DEPOSIT AND CURRENT ACCOUNT, AND IN HAND				119,342	12	10	186,062	
				£4,138,584	7	7	£4,169,048	

ASHFIELD,
E. GARCKE,
Directors.

REPORT.

with the books and vouchers of the Company and have obtained all the
subject to the sufficiency of the provisions for depreciation and renewals
up so as to exhibit a true and correct view of the state of the Company's
to us and as shown by the books of the Company.

PRICE, WATERHOUSE & CO.
DELOITTE, PLENDER, GRIFFITHS & CO.

The London and Surburban

Dr. REVENUE ACCOUNT FOR THE

	£	s	d	£	s	d	Year 1921 £
To Administration and General Expenses				2,873	2	11	3,013
,, Corporation Profits Tax				463	6	5	1,047
,, Income Tax				3,517	3	4	
,, 5 per cent. "A" Debenture Stock Service Fund				17,936	7	0	16,776
,, Interest on Debenture Stocks	19,749	8	11				
,, Interest on Deposits	6,930	16	3				
				26,680	5	2	26,216
				51,470	4	10	47,052
,, Balance, proposed to be appropriated as under—							
Dividend on 5 per cent. Cumulative Preference Shares— Balance of 4 per cent. in respect of the year 1918	64,138	4	10				
1 per cent. on account of the year 1919	16,034	11	2				
	80,172	16	0				56,121
Amount carried forward	17,243	7	7				11,523
				97,416	3	7	
				£148,886	8	5	£114,696

Traction Company, Ltd.—(*Contd.*)

Year ended 31st December 1922.   *Cr.*

	£	s	d	Year 1921 £
By Interest and Dividends from Loans and Investments ..	135,650	4	11	*110,693*
,, Sundry Receipts	1,712	11	9	*1,905*
	137,362	16	8	*112,598*
,, Balance brought forward from Last Account	11,523	11	9	*2,098*

£148,886 8 5   *£114,696*

MEADOW DAIRY
Dr. BALANCE SHEET

	£	s	d	£	s	d

To SHARE CAPITAL :
  AUTHORISED—
  700,000 7½% Cumulative Preference Shares of £1 each
	700,000	0	0			

3,600,000 Ordinary Shares of 1s. each	180,000	0	0			
	£880,000	0	0			
ISSUED— 504,737 7½% Cumulative Preference Shares of £1 each, fully paid	504,737	0	0			
3,000,000 Ordinary Shares of 1s. each, fully paid	150,000	0	0			
				654,737	0	0
,, SUNDRY CREDITORS AND CREDIT BALANCES : Trade and other Accounts	254,230	18	10			
Bills Payable	94,472	16	9			
				348,703	15	7
,, UNCLAIMED DIVIDENDS				93	6	6
,, RESERVE FUND				70,000	0	0
,, PLATE GLASS, &C., INSURANCE FUND				3,300	17	9
,, PROFIT & LOSS ACCOUNT				41,670	17	4
Contingent Liability :— *Guarantees in connection with Broughs, Limited*						
				£1,118,505	17	2

REPORT OF THE AUDITORS TO THE

We have audited the above Balance Sheet dated 7th January 1922 required. The freehold and leasehold properties and shop fixtures Ellis & Co., whilst the loose fittings at the Branches, warehouse fixtures Such valuations have been included in the above Balance Sheet and

In our opinion such Balance Sheet is properly drawn up so as to according to the best of our information and the explanations given to

Alderman's House,
  Bishopsgate, E.C.2.
    17th March 1922.

COMPANY, LIMITED.

7TH JANUARY 1922.   *Cr.*

	£	s	d	£	s	d
By Goodwill				11,606	14	7
,, Freehold and Leasehold Properties				55,567	13	2
,, Fixtures, Fittings, Plant, Machinery, Office Furniture, &c.				163,344	3	4
,, Subsidiary Companies—						
Investments	347,569	8	4			
Balance of Current Accounts, including Profits and Dividends accrued	194,939	4	10			
				542,508	13	2
,, Sundry Debtors and Debit Balances				22,676	8	10
,, Stock-in-Trade at market price or under (as certified by the Managing Directors)				226,382	14	2
,, Cash at Bankers and in hand				96,419	9	11

George Beale,
Alex Purves,
Directors.

£1,118,505 17 2

Shareholders of Meadow Dairy Co., Ltd.

and have obtained all the information and explanations we have and fittings were valued in December 1921 by Messrs. Farebrother, and plant, office furniture and motor vans were valued by the Directors. the surplus has been applied in reduction of the goodwill.

exhibit a true and correct view of the state of the Company's affairs, us and as shown by the books of the Company.

Blackburns, Barton, Mayhew & Co.
Chartered Accountants,
Auditors.

Meadow Dairy Com

PROFIT AND LOSS ACCOUNT FOR

	£	s	d
To Dividend on Preference Shares at 7½ per cent. per annum paid 30th June 1921	18,927	9	0
,, Dividend on Preference Shares at 7½ per cent. per annum paid 31st December 1921	18,927	12	9
,, Interim Dividend on Ordinary Shares of 6d. per share paid 31st December 1921	25,000	0	0
,, Amount of Profits Capitalised and Distributed in Fully-paid Ordinary Shares as per Resolution of Shareholders, 8th December 1921	100,000	0	0
,, Income Tax (including tax deducted from Profits of Subsidiary Companies)	46,731	7	5
,, Stamp Duty on New Capital	1,300	0	0
,, Reserve Fund	40,000	0	0
,, Balance as per Balance Sheet	41,670	17	4
	£292,557	6	6

pany, Ltd.—(Contd.)

THE 53 WEEKS ENDED 7TH JANUARY 1922.

	£	s	d	£	s	d
By Balance brought forward 1st January 1921	65,343	7	6			
Deduct Appropriations made by Shareholders at meeting held 4th May 1921	55,000	0	0			
				10,343	7	6
,, Profit on Trading (after charging Branch and Head Office Expenses, Managing Directors' Salaries, Directors' Fees and Depreciation of Fixtures, Fittings, &c.) for the 53 weeks ended 7th January 1922, including profits received from Subsidiary Companies				154,321	7	1
,, Profits and Dividends of Subsidiary Companies accrued, since received				127,838	4	5
. Transfer Fees				54	7	6
				£292,557	6	6

MEADOW DAIRY COMPANY, LTD.

COMBINED STATEMENT OF

	£	s	d	£	s	d
To CAPITAL—						
Meadow Dairy Co., Ltd.:						
504,737 7½% Cumulative Preference Shares of £1 each, fully paid	504,737	0	0			
3,000,000 Ordinary Shares of 1s. each, fully paid	150,000	0	0			
	654,737	0	0			
Less Shares held by Subsidiary Company	464	14	0			
	654,272	6	0			
Subsidiary Companies:						
Shares not yet acquired by Meadow Dairy Co., Ltd.	62,575	0	0			
				716,847	6	0
,, Reserve Fund:—						
Meadow Dairy Co., Ltd.				70,000	0	0
,, Reserves and Undivided Profits of Subsidiary Companies, less premiums paid by Meadow Dairy Co., Ltd., for Shares acquired				2,885	15	9
,, Proportion of Profits of Subsidiary Companies due to Outside Shareholders				2,235	3	6
,, Plate Glass, &c., Insurance Fund				3,300	17	9
,, Loans on Mortgage and Interest Accrued				89,115	17	0
,, Sundry Creditors, including Bills Payable				542,378	2	11
,, Unclaimed Dividends				168	8	10
,, Profit and Loss Account				41,670	17	4
				£1,468,602	9	1

AND SUBSIDIARY COMPANIES.
ACCOUNTS, 7TH JANUARY 1922.

	£	s	d
By Goodwill	11,606	14	7
,, Freehold and Leasehold Properties	424,605	5	4
,, Fixtures and Fittings, Plant, Machinery, Office Furniture, &c.	437,048	5	7
,, Sundry Debtors, including Payments in Advance	34,393	8	3
,, Stock-in-Trade at Market Price or under ..	426,559	8	8
,, Cash at Bankers and in Hand	134,389	6	8
	£1,468,602	9	1

THE UNDERGROUND ELECTRIC RAIL

Dr. REVENUE ACCOUNT FOR THE

	£	s	d	£	s	d	Year 1921 £
To Directors', Trustees' & Auditors' Fees, Salaries, Legal and General Office Expenses				17,687	15	4	*14,099*
,, General Interest (Net)				21,199	19	10	*11,220*
,, Income Tax				45,165	0	0	*43,089*
,, Loss on Foreign Exchange on Coupons payable abroad, including estimated provision to 31st December 1922 ..				24,230	11	7	*82,925*
,, Commission and Discount on Issue of 6% Three-Year Notes of 1923 ..				14,668	0	0	*14,668*
,, Discount on Redemption of £193,000 6% Three-Year Secured Notes				1,614	10	1	—
,, Interest at 4½% per annum on £1,832,400 4½% Bonds due 1933 ..	82,458	0	0				
Income Tax ..	29,381	11	9				
				111,839	11	9	*117,797*
,, Interest at 6 per cent. per annum on Three-Year Secured Notes, due 1923:							
To 30th June 1922, on £700,000	21,000	0	0				
To 31st December 1922, on £507,000..	15,210	0	0				
Interest accrued on £193,000 (redeemed)	1,827	2	6				
				38,037	2	6	*42,000*
		Carried forward		274,442	11	1	*325,798*

WAYS COMPANY OF LONDON, LIMITED.
YEAR ENDED 31ST DECEMBER 1922. *Cr.*

	£	s	d	Year 1921 £
BY BALANCE FROM SPECIAL RESERVE FOR EQUALISATION OF INTEREST	—			20,136
,, INCOME FROM INVESTMENTS, as per Statement (see page 167, column 10)	881,817	1	4	764,328
,, MISCELLANEOUS RECEIPTS	5,808	9	5	5,673
Carried forward	887,625	10	9	790,137

The Underground Electric Railways

		£ s. d.	£
	Brought forward	274,442 11 1	*325,798*
To AMOUNT CARRIED TO SPECIAL RESERVE for Equalisation of Interest on the 6% First Cum. Income Deb. Stock, and 6% Income Bonds		60,000 0 0	*26,242*
,, INTEREST AT 6% PER ANNUM ON £1,273,000 6% FIRST CUM. INCOME DEB. STOCK DUE 1945		76,380 0 0	*76,380*
,, INTEREST ON £6,330,050 6% INCOME BONDS DUE 1948:—			
2% for half-year ended 30th June 1922	126,601 0 0		
Income Tax	48,021 0 0		
		174,622 0 0	*180,858*
3% for half-year ended 31st Dec. 1922	189,901 10 0		
Income Tax	63,300 10 0		
		253,202 0 0	*180,859*
,, BALANCE CARRIED TO BALANCE SHEET		48,978 19 8	—
		£887,625 10 9	*790,137*

Company of London, Limited.—(*Contd.*)

Brought forward 887,625 10 9   *790,137*

£887,625 10 9   *790,137*

THE UNDERGROUND ELECTRIC RAIL

Dr. BALANCE SHEET,

Year 1921

	£ s d	£ s d	£
‡ To Share Capital: Authorised			
500,000 Shares of £10 each	5,000,000 0 0		
1,200,696 "A" Ordinary Shares of 1s. each	60,034 16 0		
	£5,060,034 16 0		
Issued			
500,000 Shares of £10 each, fully paid	5,000,000 0 0		
1,198,977 "A" Ordinary Shares of 1s. each, fully paid	59,948 17 0	5,059,948 17 0	5,059,949
* ,, 4½% Bonds of 1933 (£3,000,000 authorised)	2,948,100 0 0		
Less redeemed and cancelled	1,115,700 0 0	1,832,400 0 0	1,832,400
§ ,, 6% Three-Year Secured Notes due 1923 (£700,000 authorised)	700,000 0 0		
Less redeemed and cancelled	193,000 0 0	507,000 0 0	700,000
,, Special Reserve for Equalisation of Interest on the 6% First Cumulative Income Deb. Stock and 6% Income Bonds		86,241 10 8	26,242
† ,, 6% First Cumulative Income Debenture Stock due 1945		1,273,000 0 0	1,273,000
* ,, 6% Income Bonds due 1948 (£6,500,000 authorised)		6,330,050 0 0	6,330,050
	Carried forward	15,088,640 7 8	15,221,641

WAYS COMPANY OF LONDON, LIMITED.

31ST DECEMBER, 1922.   Cr.

	£ s d	Year 1921 £
By STOCKS AND SHARES as per Statement (see page 167, columns 5-7)	15,056,859 17 11	15,262,408
,, COMMISSION AND DISCOUNT ON ISSUE OF BONDS	428,830 6 5	428,830
,, COMMISSION AND DISCOUNT ON ISSUE OF 6% THREE-YEAR SECURED NOTES	—	14,668
,, LOANS AND INTEREST RECEIVABLE	344,956 7 0	415,525
,, INTEREST AND DIVIDENDS RECEIVABLE	349,585 10 8	265,674
,, SUNDRY DEBTORS AND DEBIT BALANCES	149,258 11 7	127,199
,, TREASURY BILLS	134,673 4 10	99,614
,, CASH AT BANKERS	9,309 0 4	115,329

Carried forward   16,473,472 18 9   16,729,247

The Underground Electric Railways

		Brought forward	15,088,640	7	8	15,221,641
To	INTEREST AND DIVIDENDS UNCLAIMED		22,594	10	3	27,002
,,	TEMPORARY LOANS ..		910,000	0	0	1,127,979
,,	SUNDRY CREDITORS AND CREDIT BALANCES ..		56,895	1	2	74,678
,,	AMOUNT PAYABLE FOR INTEREST:					
	On £1,832,400 4½% Bonds, including Income Tax	54,972 0 0				58,898
	On £1,273,000 6% First Cumulative Income Debenture Stock ..	38,190 0 0				38,190
	On £6,330,050 6% Income Bonds, including Income Tax ..	253,202 0 0				180,859
			346,364	0	0	277,947
,,	BALANCE AT CREDIT OF REVENUE ACCOUNT ..		48,978	19	8	—
			£16,473,472	18	9	16,729,247

NOTES.

‡ The profits of the Company available for dividend in respect of

As to two-thirds thereof (a) in payment of a cumulative dividend paid up on the 500,000 £10 Ordinary Shares for the time being issued, New York (as Trustees for the Contingent Certificates issued by it) per annum on the amounts paid up on the said £10 Ordinary Shares. as to one-half of the balance (if any) in payment to the Central Trust the balance as the Company thinks fit.

As to the remaining one-third thereof in payment of a dividend on

* Secured as per Trust Deed dated 30th July 1908, made between the Trust Deeds dated 1st April 1912 and 29th June 1914, made between Trustee.

§ Secured as per Trust Deed dated 8th April 1920 made between the

† Secured as per Trust Deed dated 1st April 1912, made between the and Supplemental Trust Deed dated 29th June 1914, made between

H. A. VERNET, } *Directors*.
W. M. ACKWORTH, }

We have examined the above Balance Sheet, dated 31st December all the information and explanations we have required.

We report that in our opinion such Balance Sheet is properly drawn affairs, according to the best of our information and the explanations

5 London Wall Buildings, London, E.C.2.
    26*th February* 1923.

Company of London, Limited.—(*Contd.*)

Brought forward   16,473,472   18   9   *16,729,247*

£16,473,472   18   9   *16,729,247*

each year after providing for depreciation and reserves are applicable—

at the rate of 5% per annum up to the end of such year on the amounts (*b*) subject as aforesaid in payment to the Central Trust Company of of a sum equal to a dividend for such year at the rate of 3 per cent. (*c*) subject as aforesaid in making provision for reserves, and (*d*) Company as such Trustee as aforesaid and as to the other half of

the " A " Ordinary Shares.

Company and the London & Westminster Bank, Ltd., and Supplemental the Company and the London County & Westminster Bank, Ltd., as

Company and the Union of London & Smiths Bank, Ltd., as Trustee.

Company and the Union of London and Smiths Bank, Ltd., as Trustee, the same parties.

    JNO. C. MITCHELL, *Secretary of the Company*.
    C. S. LOUCH, *Accountant of the Company*.
1922, with the Books and Vouchers of the Company, and have obtained

up so as to exhibit a true and correct view of the state of the Company's given to us, and as shown by the books of the Company.

        DELOITTE, PLENDER, GRIFFITHS & CO.,
                    Auditors.

THE UNDERGROUND ELECTRIC RAIL

Statement of Capital issued by Companies associated with amount held by the Public, by Allied Companies, and by the interest and dividends received or receivable therefrom by

* Of this £1,500,000, £537,351 is held by Trustees under Trust Deed, dated 13th January 1903, against an equal amount of Stock (Assented Stock) issued under such Deed, on which 3½% per annum is guaranteed by the Underground Electric Railways Co., of London, Ltd.
‡ This Stock is Assented Stock issued under the Trust Deed of the 13th January 1903.

§ Of this £3,000,000, £1,453,594 Undivided Ordinary Stock, £475,303, Preferred Ordinary Stock, and £619,774 ·Deferred Ordinary Stock is held by Trustees under Trust Deed dated 13th December 1912 against equal amount of Stocks (Assented Stocks) issued under such Deed, on which 4% per annum is guaranteed by the Underground Electric Railways Co. of London, Limited.

Name of Company	Total Capital Issued and Outstanding	Capital held by Public
(1)	(2)	(3)
	£	£
1. COMPANIES PARTICIPATING IN COMMON FUND—		
2. METROPOLITAN DISTRICT RAILWAY CO.	13,687,824	10,346,324
3. 3% Consolidated Rent Charge Stock	2,116,666	2,116,666
4. 4% Midland Rent Charge Stock	350,000	350,000
5. 4% Prior Lien Debenture Stock	744,586	744,586
6. 6% Debenture Stock	1,211,625	1,211,625
7. 4% Debenture Stock	1,624,200	1,624,200
8. 4% Guaranteed Stock	1,435,747	1,435,747
*9. 4½% First Preference Stock	*1,500,000	1,410,000
10. 5% Second Preference Stock	1,470,000	—
11. Ordinary Stock	3,235,000	1,453,500
12. LONDON ELECTRIC RAILWAY CO...	21,047,610	11,002,620
13. 4% Debenture Stock	5,296,000	4,864,573
14. 4½% (Redeemable) Second Debenture Stock	3,250,000	3,250,000
15. 4% Preference Stock	3,173,670	2,522,957
16. £10 Ordinary Shares	9,327,940	365,090
17. CITY & SOUTH LONDON RAILWAY CO.	6,173,829	4,301,469
18. 4% Debenture Stock	1,093,829	681,829
19. 4½% (Redeemable) Second Debenture Stock	2,750,000	2,750,000
20. 5% Preference Stocks, 1891-1903	850,000	850,000
21. Consolidated Ordinary Stock	1,480,000	19,640
22. CENTRAL LONDON RAILWAY CO...	5,014,000	5,012,500
23. 4% Debenture Stock	926,000	926,000
24. 4% (Redeemable) Debenture Stock	150,000	150,000
25. 4½% (Redeemable) Debenture Stock	458,000	458,000
26. 4½% Preference Stocks, 1902-1909	480,000	480,000
27. Ordinary Stock	3,000,000	2,998,500
28. Undivided 1,689,252		
29. Preferred 655,374		
30. Deferred 655,374		
31. §3,000,000		

WAYS COMPANY OF LONDON, LIMITED.—(Contd.)

the Underground Electric Railways Co. of London, Ltd., showing the Underground Electric Railways Co. of London, Ltd., together with the the Underground Co.

	Capital held by U. E. R. Co. of L., Ltd.				Interest and Dividends received or receivable by U. E. R. Co. of L., Ltd.		
Capital held by Allied Companies	Deposited with Trustees under various Trust Deeds	Amount of Free Assets	Total	Percentage of Total held by U.E.R. Co.	1922.		1921
					Rate per c't. per annum	Amount	Rate per c't. per annum
(4)	(5)	(6)	(7)	(8)	(9)	(10)	(11)
£	£	£	£			£ s d	
..	..	..	3,341,500	..	..	130,095 0 0	..
..	..	..	..	..	..	..	..
..	..	..	..	..	..	..	..
..	..	..	..	..	..	..	..
..	..	..	..	..	..	..	..
..	‡90,000	..	‡90,000	6.00	3½	3,150 0 0	3½
..	1,470,000	..	1,470,000	100.00	5	73,500 0 0	5
..	1,781,500	..	1,781,500	55.07	3	53,445 0 0	1
..	..	..	10,044,990	..	..	410,853 14 6	..
..	431,000	427	431,427	..	4	26,311 1 8	4
..	650,466	247	650,713	20.51	4	26,028 10 4	4
..	7,900,020	†1,062,830	8,962,850	96.09	4	358,514 2 6	3¼
..	..	..	1,872,360	..	..	74,894 8 0	..
..	412,000	..	412,000	37.67	4	16,480 0 0	4
..	..	..	..	..	..	..	..
..	1,460,360	..	1,460,360	98.67	4	58,414 8 0	3¼
..	..	..	1,500	..	..	60 0 0	..
..	..	..	..	..	..	..	..
..	..	..	..	..	..	..	..
..	..	..	..	..	..	..	..
..	..	1,500	1,500	.05	4	60 0 0	4

The Underground Electric Railways

† Lodged with the National Provincial and Union Bank of England, Ltd., as collateral security against loan of £600,000 under Agreement dated 19th July 1921.

32. London General Omnibus Co., Ltd.	4,680,211	2,469,731
33. 4½% First Debenture Stock	1,349,731	1,349,731
34. 5% Cum. Income Debenture Stock	1,130,000	1,120,000
35. £10 Ordinary Shares	2,200,480	..
36. Total for Companies Participating in Common Fund	50,603,474	33,132,644
37. Per cent. of Total Capital Issued and Outstanding	..	65.47%
38. London & Suburban Traction Co., Ltd.	3,863,909	2,866,319
39. 4½% First Mortgage Debenture Stock	182,635	182,635
40. 5% Debenture Stock	231,713	227,013
41. 5% £1 Cumulative Preference Shares	1,603,456	1,401,120
42. £1 Ordinary Shares	1,846,105	1,055,551
43. London & Suburban Traction Co., Ltd. (Associated Companies).		
44. Metropolitan Electric Tramways, Ltd.	1,667,959	747,341
45. 4½% Debenture Stock	445,449	445,449
46. 5% Debenture Stock	248,174	248,174
47. 5% £1 Cumulative Preference Shares	500,000	43,333
48. £1 Ordinary Shares	474,336	10,385
49. London United Tramways, Ltd.	2,476,932	1,769,108
50. 4% First Mortgage Debenture Stock	857,841	857,841
51. 5% £1 Preference Shares	962,841	812,091
52. 5s. Ordinary Shares	656,250	99,176
53. Tramways (M.E.T.) Omnibus Co., Ld.	236,950	126,950
54. 4½% Debenture Stock	126,950	126,950
55. 7% £1 Cumulative Preference Shares	100,000	..
56. £1 Ordinary Shares, 1s. paid	10,000	..
57. South Metropolitan Electric Tramways & Lighting Co., Ltd.	479,550	130,114
58. 4% 1st Mortgage Debenture Stock	128,791	128,791
59. 6% £1 Cumulative Preference Shares	169,569	1,323
60. £1 Ordinary Shares	181,190	..
61. Total for London & Suburban Traction Co., Ltd., and Associated Co.'s	8,725,300	5,639,832
62. Per cent. of Total Capital Issued and Outstanding	..	64.64%

Company of London.—(Contd.)

	10,000	..	..	2,200,480	..	..	253,614 12 10	..
	..	..	..	..	..	..	..	..
L.G.O.	10,000	..	..	..	..	8½	187,040 16 0	8
	..	1,600,480	†600,000	2,200,480	100.00	Free of Tax	66,573 16 10	Free of Tax
	10,000	..	..	17,460,830	..	..	869,517 15 4	..
	.02%	..	..	34.51%	..	..	..	..
	101,280	..	..	896,310	..	..	7,599 6 0	..
M.E.T.	4,700	..	..	..	..	..	..	..
{ L.U.T.	50,100 }							
	250 }	76,885	75,101	151,986	9.48	5	7,599 6 0	3½
{ M.E.T.	46,000 }							
L.U.T.	230 }	420,734	323,590	744,324	40.32	..	..	..
	920,618	..	..	..	..	..	..	..
	..	..	..	..	..	..	..	..
L. & S.T.	456,667	..	..	..	..	..	..	..
,,	463,951	..	..	..	..	..	..	..
	673,517	..	..	34,307	..	..	..	..
L. & S.T.	116,443	..	34,307	34,307	3.56	..	..	..
,,	557,074	..	..	..	..	..	..	..
	110,000	..	..	..	..	..	..	..
	..	..	..	..	..	..	..	..
L.G.O.	100,000	..	..	..	..	..	..	..
L. & S.T.	10,000	..	..	..	..	..	..	..
	349,436	..	..	..	..	..	..	..
	..	..	..	..	..	..	..	..
L. & S.T.	168,246	..	..	..	..	..	..	..
,,	181,190	..	..	..	..	..	..	..
	2,154,851	..	..	930,617	..	..	7,599 6 0	..
	24.69%	..	..	10.67%	..	..	..	..

The Underground Electric Railways

63. ASSOCIATED EQUIPMENT CO., LTD.	1,100,000	..
64. £10 Ordinary Shares	1,100,000	..
65. Per cent. of TOTAL CAPITAL Issued and Outstanding ..	..	..
66. OTHER ALLIED COMPANIES—		
67. WIMBLEDON & SUTTON RAILWAY CO.	5,350	2,930
68. £10 Ordinary Shares	5,350	2,930
69. UNION SURPLUS LANDS CO., LTD.	250,000	..
70. 4% Debentures	100,000	..
71. £1 Ordinary Shares ..	150,000	..
72. UNION CONSTRUCTION CO., LTD.	980	..
73. £20 Shares. 37 fully paid ..	740	..
74. 120 £2 paid	240	..
75. WATFORD & EDGWARE RAILWAY CO. ..	518	102
76. Shares £2 paid	518	102
77. WHITECHAPEL & BOW RAILWAY CO. ..	1,559,000	959,000
78. 4% Debenture Stock	359,000	359,000
79. £10 Ordinary Shares	1,200,000	600,000
80. TOTAL FOR ALLIED COMPANIES ..	1,815,848	962,032
81. Per cent. of TOTAL CAPITAL Issued and Outstanding ..	..	52.98%
82. TOTALS ..	£62,244,622	£39,734,508
83. PER CENT. OF TOTAL CAPITAL ISSUED AND OUTSTANDING	..	63.84%

84. TOTALS AS SHOWN ABOVE ..	..	..	..	..	..
85. METROPOLITAN RAILWAY CO. Consolidated Ordinary Stock	..	..	..	..	
86. ..	..	..	..	..	..
87. ..	..	..	..	..	..

Company of London.—(Contd.)

	500,000	..	..	600,000	..	..	..		..
L.G.O.	500,000	100,000	500,000	600,000	54.55	..	..		..
	45.45%	..	..	54.55%	..	..	..		..
	..	..	..	2,420	..	..	..		..
	..	..	2,420	2,420	45.23	..	..		..
	..	..	..	250,000	..	..	4,000	0 0	..
	..	..	100,000	100,000	100.00	4	4,000	0 0	4
	..	..	150,000	150,000	100.00	..	..		..
	..	..	..	980	..	..	..		..
	..	..	740	740	100.00	..	..		..
	..	..	240	240	100.00	..	..		..
	..	..	..	416	..	..	..		..
	..	..	416	416	80.31	..	..		..
	600,000	..	..	..	..	..	..		..
M.D.R.	600,000	..	..	..	..	..	..		..
	600,000	..	..	253,816	..	..	4,000	0 0	..
	33.014%	..	..	13.98%	..	..	..		..
	3,264,851	16,393,445	2,851,818	19,245,263	..	..	881,117	1 4	..
	5.24%	..	..	30.92%	..	..	..		..

..	..	..	16,393,445	2,851,818	19,245,263	..	..	..		..
..	..	..	..	20,000	20,000	..	3½	700 0 0		2¼
..	..	..	16,393,445	2,871,818	19,265,263	..	..	881,817 1 4		..
..	..	..		Book Value £15,056,860				(See Revenue		A/c.)
				(See Balance Sheet).						

I.

UNITED BRITISH OILFIELDS
And Subsidiary Companies

Dr. CONSOLIDATED PROFIT AND LOSS ACCOUNT

	£	s	d
Stocks of Oil at 1st Jan. 1921	29,986	2	1
Cost of Production, Refining, and Transportation, including Royalties, Administration, and General Expenses, Maintenance, Sales, Commissions, &c., less Interest on Loans	144,287	4	6
Purchase of Crude and Fuel Oils	8,467	1	0
On Account of Depreciation	31,895	1	6
Preliminary Formation and Legal Expenses, written off	25,388	17	10
Unproductive and Abandoned Wells, Amount written off	6,462	4	3
Lorries, Cars, &c., Amount written off	5,296	3	3
Reserve for Corporation Profits Tax	1,000	0	0
Balance carried to Balance Sheet	5,337	8	11
	£258,120	3	4

CONSOLIDATED BALANCE

	£	s	d	£	s	d
To Capital Authorised— 1,500,000 Shares of £1 each	1,500,000	0	0			
,, Capital Issued— 1,500,000 Shares of £1 each fully paid				1,500,000	0	0
,, Drafts Payable against Cash received in Trinidad				5,500	0	0
,, Sundry Creditors and Outstandings— London	32,094	15	8			
Trinidad	10,749	19	3			
				42,844	14	11
Carried forward				1,548,344	14	11

OF TRINIDAD, LIMITED,
Wholly Owned.

FOR THE YEAR ENDING 31ST DECEMBER 1921.   *Cr.*

	£	s	d
Proceeds of Sales and Oil Consumed as Fuel..	237,652	6	8
Received for Transportation of Oil, and Working of Pipelines	1,093	9	8
Stocks of Oil at 31st Dec. 1921..	19,374	7	0
	£258,120	3	4

SHEET AT 31ST DECEMBER 1921.

	£ s d	£	s	d
By Purchase of Undertaking of Trinidad Oilfields, Ltd., including Lands, Oil and Mineral Rights, Property, &c., cost of purchase of the United British West Indies Petroleum Syndicate, Ltd., investments of that Syndicate in the United British Producing Co., Ltd., and the United British Mineral Oil Co., Ltd., and loans for Development to the United British Producing Co., Ltd., and to the United British Mineral Oil Co., Ltd.		813,118	9	5
Carried forward		813,118	9	5

United British Oilfields

	Brought forward		1,548,344 14 11
To Profit and Loss Account— Profit for the year 1921 (subject to Provision for Income Tax, if any) ..	5,337 8 11		
Less Adverse Balance, as per last Balance Sheet..	2,005 17 6		
		3,331 11 5

Carried forward 1,551,676 6 4

of Trinidad, Limited.—(Contd.)

		Brought forward		813,118 9 5	
By Expenditure on Properties since the date of purchase of Undertaking of the Trinidad Oilfields, Ltd. :—					
Wells Drilled .. £261,344 11 7					
Less Written Off on account of abandoned and unproductive wells in previous years .. 46,502 1 0					
Add for the year 1921 .. 6,462 4 3					
52,964 5 3					
		208,380 6 4			
Wells Drilling and in course of Preparation		27,653 6 1			
Collecting Lines, Steam Plant, Storage, &c.		60,697 4 3			
Drilling Tools		37,822 19 2			
Roads, Buildings, Water Supply, &c.		80,128 5 7			
Furniture, Fittings, &c.		8,148 8 10			
Lorries, Cars, &c., as revalued by the Management in Trinidad ..		4,906 15 3			
		427,737 5 6			
Less on Account of Depreciation in previous years.. .. £70,000 0 0					
Add for the year 1921 20,000 0 0					
		90,000 0 0			
				337,737 5 6	
,, Capital Expenditure on Refinery Undertaking		99,632 16 6			
Less Depreciation		10,635 12 5			
				88,997 4 1	
		Carried forward		1,239,852 19 0	

United British Oilfields

Brought forward 1,551,676 6 4

£1,551,676 6 4

NOTE.—The Assets and Liabilities of the United British West Indies Petroleum Syndicate, Ltd., (the whole of the capital of which is held by the United British Oilfields of Trinidad, Ltd.), and the Assets and Liabilities of the United British Refineries, Ltd. and United British Pipelines, Ltd. (the whole of the capital of each of which is held by the United British West Indies Petroleum Syndicate, Ltd.), are included in the above figures, under their respective headings.

COCHRANE OF CULTS, } *Directors*.
R. WALEY COHEN,

TO THE SHAREHOLDERS OF THE UNITED

We report that we have examined the above Consolidated Balance Companies in London, and with the returns received from Trinidad, required. The expenditure charged to Capital Accounts is based on the inspected the Deeds of Properties which we understand are held in provision for Depreciation, the above Consolidated Balance Sheet is gate state of affairs of the four combined Companies, according to the by the books and vouchers of the Companies in London, and the

3 Frederick's Place,
Old Jewry, E.C.2.
12*th* *October* 1922.

of Trinidad, Limited.—(Contd.)

			Brought forward	1,239,852 19 0
By	Capital Expenditure on Pipeline Undertaking		13,353 16 0	
	Less Depreciation		1,123 16 7	
				12,229 19 5
,,	Miscellaneous Assets of the United British West Indies PetroleumSyndicate Ltd.		1,928 14 9	
	Less Depreciation		135 12 6	
				1,793 2 3
,,	Elsidore Estate at Cost			8,394 5 0
,,	Stocks on Hand—Trinidad : Stores and Sundry Stocks as valued by the Management in Trinidad		215,336 18 1	
	Stores in Transit		1,266 6 9	
	Stocks of Oil		19,374 7 0	
				235,977 11 10
,,	Sundry Debtors and Prepayments :			
	London		5,635 18 11	
	Trinidad		10,844 8 11	
				16,480 7 10
,,	Special Deposit			24,000 0 0
,,	Cash at Bank and in Hand : Trinidad and London			12,948 1 0
				£1,551,676 6 4

BRITISH OILFIELDS OF TRINIDAD, LIMITED.

Sheet, dated 31st December 1921, with the books and vouchers of the and have obtained all the information and explanations we have allocation of expenditure received from Trinidad. We have not Trinidad. We are of opinion that, subject to the sufficiency of the properly drawn up so as to exhibit a true and correct view of the aggrebest of our information, and the explanations given to us, and as shown aforementioned returns from Trinidad.

PRICE, WATERHOUSE & CO.,
Chartered Accountants,
Auditors.

VAN DEN

BALANCE SHEET,

LIABILITIES.	£	s	d			
NOMINAL & ISSUED CAPITAL:						
90,000 Cumulative 6% Preference Shares of £5 each	450,000	0	0			
1,000,000 Cumulative 6% " B " Preference Shares of £1 each	1,000,000	0	0			
1,000,000 Cumulative 7% " C " Preference Shares of £1 each	1,000,000	0	0			
3,750,000 15% Preferred Ordinary Shares (non-cumulative) of 5s. each	937,500	0	0			
750,000 Ordinary Shares of 5s. each	187,500	0	0			
				3,575,000	0	0
BILLS PAYABLE				598,839	11	10
SUNDRY CREDITORS AND OUTSTANDINGS				874,787	7	4
Do. Associated and Subsidiary Companies secured against Stocks of Raw Materials				96,705	0	2
RESERVE FUND as at 31st December 1920	500,000	0	0			
PROFIT & LOSS ACCOUNT: Balance as shown in General Profit and Loss Account	166,566	2	10			
				666,566	2	10

(Subject to provision for depreciation in Exchange in respect of assets of Associated Companies.)

Contingent Liabilities: On Bills discounted, £250,838; On Bank Overdrafts Guaranteed, £21,084; On Forward Contracts (most of which have since run off) £1,004,737.

There are also Contingent liabilities in respect of a guarantee of Preference Shares of a Dutch Associated Company and a mutual guarantee of the Preference and Ordinary Shares of another Dutch Associated Company.

Carried forward	5,811,898	2	2

BERGHS, LIMITED.

31st December, 1921.

	Assets. £	s	d	£	s	d
Goodwill Account				656,462	17	2
Freehold and Leasehold Land and Buildings, *less* Depreciation	370,588	0	9			
Plant, Machinery & Utensils, *less* Depreciation	245,296	1	9			
Rolling Stock, Furniture, &c., *less* Depreciation	30,055	19	4			
				645,940	1	10
Associated and Subsidiary Companies:						
Holdings, including Goodwill therein	1,511,057	19	3			
Current Account Balances	554,849	2	2			
				2,065,907	1	5
Sundry Debtors, Loans and Payments in Advance (*less* Reserves) including £407,233 Claims in respect of ex-Enemy pre-war debts still before the British Clearing Office				1,178,213	14	4
Stocks of Raw Materials and Manufactured Goods as certified by the Company's Officials (exclusive of Raw Materials purchased but not delivered)	724,117	14	4			
Stocks of Stores, Packages, &c., as certified by the Company's Officials	31,668	6	8			
				755,786	1	0
Bills Receivable				6,255	1	11
Cash at Bankers and in Hand				197,131	18	6
Investments:						
War Stocks, &c.	65,653	16	8			
Trade and Sundries	83,645	6	8			
				149,299	3	4
		Carried forward		5,654,995	19	6

Van Den Berghs,

Brought forward 5,811,898 2 2

£5,811,898 2 2

To THE SHAREHOLDERS OF

We report that we have examined the above Balance Sheet, dated all the information and explanations we have required.   We have also Associated Companies abroad.

The Assets and Liabilities include certain estimates of sums due to but which it has not yet been possible to verify.

Subject to this, we are of the opinion that the above Balance Sheet state of the Company's affairs according to the best of our information Company.

3 Frederick's Place, London, E.C.2.
    26th *September* 1922.

Limited.—(Contd.)

Brought forward	5,654,995	19	6
Reserve Fund Investments (War Loan, Colonial Stocks, Leasehold Office Buildings in London, &c.)	106,651	3	9
Expenditure carried forward to be written off in succeeding years	50,250	18	11

Henry Van den Bergh,
Walter Townley,
  Directors.
A. G. Hales, *Secretary.*

£5,811,898 2 2

Van den Berghs, Limited.

31st December 1921, with the Books of the Company, and have obtained audited the Balance Sheets as at 31st December 1921 of the principal

and by the Company, which we are satisfied have been reasonably made,

is properly drawn up so as to exhibit a true and correct view of the and the explanations given to us, and as shown by the books of the

Price, Waterhouse & Co.,
Chartered Accountants.

Van den Berghs,

Dr. GENERAL PROFIT AND LOSS ACCOUNT

	£ s d	£ s d	£ s d
Loss for year to date after taking into account Dividends and Distribution satisfied in Shares of Associated Companies, Profits and Losses of Subsidiary Companies, and Income from Trade and Reserve Investments			176,866 13 1
Depreciation			42,849 2 7
Directors' and Managing Directors' Remuneration			37,168 11 6
Dividends Paid :—			
On Preference Shares to 31st August 1921	27,000 0 0		
Less amount provided for in Appropriation Account, 31st December 1920..	9,000 0 0		
		18,000 0 0	
On " B " Preference Shares to 31st December 1921..		60,000 0 0	
On " C " Preference Shares to 30th November 1921..	70,000 0 0		
Less amount provided for in Appropriation Account, 31st December 1920..	5,833 6 8		
		64,166 13 4	
On Preferred Ordinary Shares to 30th June 1921..	140,625 0 0		
Less amount provided for in Appropriation Account, 31st December 1920	70,312 10 0		
		70,312 10 0	
			212,479 3 4
Balance carried to Balance Sheet			166,566 2 10
(Subject to provision for depreciation in Exchange in respect of assets of Associated Companies.)			
			£635,929 13 4

Limited.—(Contd.)

FOR THE YEAR ENDED 31ST DECEMBER 1921. Cr.

	£ s d	£ s d
Balance 31st December 1920		800,531 16 0
Less—		
Amounts appropriated at 31st December 1920 :—		
Accrued proportion of Preference Dividend to 31st December 1920	9,000 0 0	
Accrued proportion of " C " Preference Dividend to 31st December 1920	5,833 6 8	
6 months' Dividend on 3,750,000 Preferred Ordinary Shares	70,312 10 0	
Final Dividend of 4/- per Share on 750,000 Ordinary Shares	150,000 0 0	
	235,145 16 8	
Less Income-tax	70,543 14 0	
		164,602 2 8
		635,929 13 4

£635,929 13 4

VICKERS

Dr.   BALANCE SHEET

CAPITAL ACCOUNT.
AUTHORISED—
£750,000 Preferred 5 per cent. Stock
£750,000 5 per cent. Preference Shares of £1 each
£7,000,000 5 per cent. Cum'lative Preference Shares of £1 each (free of Tax up to 6s. in the £)
£18,000,000 Ordinary Shares of £1 each

£26,500,000

	£ s d	£ s d
ISSUED:		
Shares: 12,315,483 Ordinary Shares of £1 each fully paid	12,315,483 0 0	
6,863,807 5 per cent. Cumulative Preference Shares of £1 each, fully paid	6,863,807 0 0	
750,000 5 per cent. Preference Shares of £1 each, all paid	750,000 0 0	
Stock: Preferred 5 per cent. Stock	750,000 0 0	
		20,679,290 0 0
4 PER CENT. FIRST MORTGAGE DEBENTURE STOCK	1,250,000 0 0	
Interest Accrued	2,972 12 0	
		1,252,972 12 0
7 PER CENT. SEVEN YEAR NOTES: Authorised: £4,000,000 Issued	1,500,000 0 0	
Add Interest accrued	36,750 0 0	
		1,536,750 0 0
	Carried forward	23,469,012 12 0

LIMITED.

AT 31ST DECEMBER 1921.   *Cr.*

	£ s d	£ s d
LAND, BUILDINGS, MACHINERY, TOOLS, PLANT, &C., at 31st December 1920	7,570,659 19 5	
Additions, *less* Sales, for year ended 31st December 1921	89,813 18 5	7,660,473 17 10
INTERESTS IN SUBSIDIARY AND CONNECTED COMPANIES		18,144,967 6 4
MARKETABLE SECURITIES		1,044,463 14 2
STOCK OF STEEL, IRON, TIMBER AND OTHER MATERIALS, and WORK IN PROGRESS, *less* instalments		2,669,329 5 10
SUNDRY BOOK DEBTS OWING TO THE COMPANY		6,213,703 12 8
CASH AND BILLS IN HAND		1,620,345 7 2

Carried forward   7,353,283 4 0

Vickers

Brought forward				23,469,012	12	0
CREDITORS, INCLUDING £370,000 SECURED LOANS AND PROVISION FOR FINAL PREFERENCE DIVIDENDS FOR YEAR TO 31ST DECEMBER 1921				6,084,364	7	7
RESERVE ACCOUNTS:						
Premiums on Shares	2,042,593	18	0			
Works Reserve Account	3,200,000	0	0			
General Reserve Account	1,200,000	0	0			
War Risks Insurance	53,276	18	2			
				6,495,870	16	2
PROFIT AND LOSS ACCOUNT: Net Profit for year ended 31st December 1921 after allowing for adjustments of reserves for Taxation	708,102	15	10			
Add Brought forward from 31st December 1920	991,639	3	11			
	1,699,741	19	9			
Less PREFERENCE DIVIDENDS FOR THE YEAR 1921	395,706	11	6			
				1,304,035	8	3
				£37,353,283	4	0

NOTE.—Contingent Liabilities in respect of the Company's guarantees as under :—
(1) Of £898,200 6% Debentures issued by Canadian Vickers, Ltd.
(2) Of Bankers' Loans and Overdrafts, and Contract guarantees up to £824,152 for Subsidiary and Associated Concerns, &c.

AUDITORS'
We have audited the above Balance Sheet and have obtained all the
The Stock-in-Trade has been certified by responsible officials of the prices. The additions to Buildings, Machinery and Plant have been
The Investments in Subsidiary and Connected Companies are taken in Marketable Securities are in the aggregate below their market value.
There are some matters still to be adjusted arising in connection with
In our opinion the above Balance Sheet is properly drawn up so as according to the best of our information and the explanations given to

5th July 1922.

Limited.—(Contd.)

Brought forward 37,353,283 4 0

DOUGLAS VICKERS,
V. CAILLARD,
   Directors.

           £37,353,283 4 0

REPORT.

information and explanations we have required.

Company to be valued at or under cost, and not exceeding market approved by the Board, and details thereof have been laid before us.

at their book values, in no case exceeding cost; and the Investments

Government accounts.

to exhibit a true and correct view of the state of the Company's affairs us and as shown by the Books of the Company.

          W. B. PEAT & Co.,
            Auditors.

INTERNATIONAL HARVESTER COMPANY AND AFFILIATED COMPANIES.

INCOME ACCOUNT FOR 1922.

Income before deducting Interest on Loans, Depreciation, and Provision for Losses on Receivables		$11,417,484.17
Deduct:		
Interest on Loans	$916,812.39	
Ore and Timber Depletion	330,021.27	
Plant Depreciation	3,455,601.76	
Special Maintenance	183,773.20	
Provision for Losses on Receivables	990,507.62	
		5,876,716.24
Net Profit of International Harvester Company and Affiliated Companies		$5,540,767.93

SURPLUS, 31ST DECEMBER 1922.

Balance at 31st December 1921		$59,526,787.52
Add:		
Net Profit for 1922		5,540,767.93
		$65,067,555.45
Deduct:		
Cash Dividends:		
Preferred Stock, $7 per share	$4,215,673.00	
Common Stock, $5 per share	4,847,920.00	
	$9,063,593.00	
Stock Dividends—2% semi-annually	3,802,290.00	
		12,865,883.00
Surplus of International Harvester Company and Affiliated Companies		$52,201,672.45

INTERNATIONAL HARVESTER COM
COMBINED BALANCE SHEET,

Assets.

Property :
Real Estate, Plant Property,
Mines, Timber Lands, &c. $117,275,835.41
  Deduct :
  Reserves for Plant Depreciation 32,106,018.13
                                                                $85,169,817.28

Deferred Charges 376,608.92

Pension Fund Securities ..   4,410,373.76

Current Assets :
  Inventories :
    Raw Materials, Work in Process, Finished Products, &c. $87,810,483.98
  Receivables :
    Dealers' and Farmers' Notes $48,791,151.43
    Accounts Receivable 21,738,892.02
                         $70,530,043.45
    Deduct :
    Reserves for Losses   4,721,720.66
                                        65,808,322.79
  Cash 10,892,986.54
                                                                 164,511,793.31
                                                                 ─────────────
                                                                $254,468,593.27

---

* *Here follows a report setting out details*

PANY AND AFFILIATED COMPANIES.

31st December, 1922.

Liabilities.

Capital Stock:	Authorised	Issued	
Preferred	$100,000,000	$60,223,900	
Common	130,000,000	97,918,404	
			$158,142,304.00
Current Liabilities:			
Bills Payable:			
Foreign Trade Acceptances		$5,635,000.00	
Accounts Payable:			
Current Invoices, Payrolls, Taxes, &c. $12,876,923.92			
Preferred Stock Dividend 1,053,918.25			
Common Stock Dividend 1,223,980.00			
		15,154,822.17	
			20,789,822.17
Reserves (Appropriated Surplus):			
Special Maintenance		$2,624,308.07	
Collection Expenses		2,000,000.00	
Fire Insurance Fund		7,747,873.50	
Pension Fund		6,762,613.08	
Industrial Accident Fund		950,000.00	
Contingent		3,250,000.00	
			23,334,794.65
Surplus			52,201,672.45
			$254,468,593.27

of the figures in the above Balance Sheet.

The Board of Directors
    International Harvester Company,
        Chicago, Illinois.

 We have audited the books, accounts and records of the International Harvester Company and of its affiliated companies located in the United States and Canada, and have examined the annual reports of affiliated companies located in other countries, for the year ended 31st December 1922.

 We have examined the charges to capital accounts, have verified the cash and other current assets at 31st December 1922, including the inventories of raw materials and supplies, work in process, and finished products, and have verified the Income and Profit and Loss Accounts.

 We find that the Company has valued raw materials and supplies, work in process of manufacture and finished products at cost or market, whichever was lower, and has made adequate provision for depreciation of inventory items.

 The Company has pursued a conservative policy in its charges to capital accounts, has valued its foreign current assets at prevailing exchange rates, or less, has set up adequate reserves for depreciation and for possible losses, and has made provision for all known liabilities.

 WE HEREBY CERTIFY that, in our opinion, the Combined Balance Sheet and the Income Account submitted herewith, reflect the true financial condition at 31st December 1922, and the results from operations for the year.

HASKINS & SELLS.

Chicago, Illinois,
  1st March 1923.

INTERNATIONAL MERCANTILE MARINE COMPANY AND SUBSIDIARY COMPANIES.

STATEMENT OF EARNINGS FOR THE YEARS ENDED RESPECTIVELY 31ST DECEMBER 1921, 31ST DECEMBER 1920, and 31ST DECEMBER 1919, FROM THE OPERATIONS OF THE AMERICAN, RED STAR, WHITE STAR, ATLANTIC TRANSPORT AND LEYLAND LINES AND DIVIDENDS FROM PARTLY-OWNED COMPANIES.

	*1921	*1920	*1919
Gross Voyage Earnings	$90,068,417.89	$113,331,818.54	$58,875,493.97
Miscellaneous Earnings	8,027,609.97	12,475,634.37	8,751,473.69
	$98,096,027.86	$125,807,452.91	$67,626,967.66
Operating and General Expenses, Taxes and Miscellaneous Charges	85,094,107.60	110,387,584.45	47,139,690.60
	$13,001,920.26	$15,419,868.46	$20,487,277.06
Fixed Charges	2,623,262.11	2,637,690.31	2,737,345.33
Profit for the Year, before providing for Depreciation on Steamships	$10,378,658.15	$12,782,178.15	$17,749,931.73

Profit for year 1921, before providing for Depreciation on Steamships, as shown above	$10,378,658.15
Deduct: Depreciation on Steamships for 1921	6,117,980.50
Surplus for the Year 1921	$4,260,677.65
Add: Surplus, 31st December 1920	30,556,973.08
	$34,817,650.73

Deduct:
Dividends on I.M.M. Co. Preferred Stock:

Declared	Paid	Rate	Amount	
June 9, 1921	Aug. 1, 1921	3% Semi-annual	$1,551,765.00	
Dec. 15, 1921	Feb. 1, 1922	3% Semi-annual	1,551,750.00	
				3,103,515.00

Surplus as shown by Balance Sheet, Dec. 31, 1921	$31,714,135.73

* For 1921 and 1920 the earnings as shown include the entire earnings of Leyland Line. For 1919 the figures stated include only that portion of Leyland Line earnings received in dividends by International Mercantile Marine Co.

INTERNATIONAL MERCANTILE MARINE COMPANY.

INSURANCE FUND—INCOME ACCOUNT—Year Ended 31st December 1921.

	Dollars		Dollars
Gross Premiums paid into the Fund	$3,240,657.53	Lay-up and Cancellation Returns	$802,059.46
Interest Received	153,631.59	Premiums paid for Insurance with Outside Underwriters and Losses less Recoveries	1,779,886.45
		Expenses and Taxes	237,671.13
		Interest paid	66,630.14
		Difference in Exchange	61,516.20
		Profit for the Year	446,525.74
	$3,394,289.12		$3,394,289.12

We have examined the above Statement of Earnings and Expenses of the Insurance Fund of the International Mercantile Marine Company for the year ended 31st December 1921, and certify that the same is correct. Full provision has been made therein for all claims in respect of losses during the year, so far as they are known or can be estimated. The transactions in £ sterling are converted at the rate of 4.85 per £.

PRICE, WATERHOUSE & CO.

56 Pine Street, New York.
1st *July* 1922.

INTERNATIONAL MERCANTILE MARINE
Comprising American, Red Star, White Star,
CONSOLIDATED BALANCE SHEET,

Assets.

Capital Assets—		
Cost of Properties :*		
Balance at 31st December 1920	$232,861,403.67	
Additions during the year 1921, and advances on account of new construction *less* steamships sold and gone out of service	12,245,384.74	
	$245,106,788.41	
Less—Reserve for Depreciation	56,387,728.54	
		$188,719,059.87
*Combined undertakings and their properties at cost to International Mercantile Marine Company in Bonds, Stocks and Cash.		
Investments in Sundry Shipping and other Companies, Exchange Memberships and Government Deposits		7,234,755.41
Total Capital Assets		$195,953,815.28
Current Assets—		
Inventories	$2,138,745.00	
Accounts Receivable	10,545,927.17	
Bills Receivable and Loans	1,358,000.00	
Interest Receivable and Accrued	381,292.26	
Agency Balances	565,376.15	
Marketable Stocks and Bonds, &c.	47,717,190.55	
Cash at Bankers, on Hand and in Transit	9,970,556.82	
Total Current Assets		72,677,087.95
Deferred Charges to Profit and Loss		7,298,760.49
	Carried forward	275,929,663.72

COMPANY and Subsidiary Companies.
ATLANTIC TRANSPORT AND LEYLAND LINES.
31ST DECEMBER, 1921.

LIABILITIES.

CAPITAL LIABILITIES :			
Capital Stock :			
Preferred†	$60,000,000.00		
Less—In Treasury	8,275,000.00		
		$51,725,000.00	
Common	$60,000,000.00		
Less—In Treasury	10,128,200.00		
		49,871,800.00	
			$101,596,800.00
†Accumulated dividends unpaid, 42 per cent.			
Capital Stock of Frederick Leyland & Co., Ltd., held by Public			27,645.00
Bonds and Debentures :			
First Mortgage and Collateral Trust Six per cent. Gold Bonds		$40,000,000.00	
Less—In			
Treasury	$500,000.00		
Retired by Sinking Fund	2,187,000.00		
		2,687,000.00	
		$37,313,000.00	
Debenture Bonds of Oceanic Steam Navigation Co., Ltd., held by Public		7,839,540.00	
			45,152,540.00
Loans on Mortgage			1,500,000.00
Total Capital Liabilities			$148,276,985.00
CURRENT LIABILITIES :			
Loans, Bills Payable and Foreign Bank Overdrafts		$8,890,493.70	
Accounts Payable, including Reserves for United States and Foreign Taxes		29,146,911.08	
Interest Payable and Accrued		677,036.88	
Agency Balances		1,027,037.86	
Preferred Stock Dividend Payable 1st February 1922		1,551,750.00	
Reserve for Liabilities		8,666,892.08	
			49,960,121.60
		Carried forward	198,237,106.60

International Mercantile Marine Com

Brought forward   275,929,663.72

$275,929,663.72

We have examined the books and accounts of the International
the American, Red Star, White Star, Atlantic Transport, and Leyland
Sheet of 31st December 1921 and the relative statement of earnings
therefrom.
We have verified the cash. and securities by actual inspection or by
full provision has been made for bad and doubtful accounts receivable
The accounts of the British subsidiary companies are included in
i.e. $4.85 per £.
Upon the above basis, we certify that in our opinion the consolidated
position of the Companies on 31st December 1921, and the relative
the operations for the twelve months ending that date.
56 Pine Street,
    New York.
       1st *July* 1922.

pany and Subsidiary Companies.—(Contd.)

		Brought forward	198,237,106.60
MISCELLANEOUS RESERVES	..		32,648,552.87
DEFERRED CREDITS TO PROFIT AND LOSS	.. .. ..		11,296,374.70
INSURANCE FUND :			
Balance, 1st January 1921	..	1,586,968.08	
Profit for year 1921	..	446,525.74	
			2,033,493.82
SURPLUS ..	.. .. ..		31,714,135.73

$275,929,663.72

Mercantile Marine Company and its subsidiary companies, comprising Lines, for the year 1921, and we find that the consolidated Balance for the twelve months ending that date have been correctly prepared

certificates from the depositaries and we have satisfied ourselves that and for all ascertainable liabilities.
the consolidated statements at the Companies' standard rate of exchange,

balance sheet is properly drawn up so as to show the true financial statement of earnings is a fair and correct summary of the results of

PRICE, WATERHOUSE & CO.

IRON PRODUCTS CORPORA
CONSOLIDATED BALANCE SHEET AND

Assets.

PATENTS AND GOOD WILL		$1.00
LAND, BUILDINGS, PLANT EQUIPMENT AND MINERAL RIGHTS ..	$13,195,827.78	
Less Reserves for Depreciation, Amortisation, Depletion, and minority interest in The Central Foundry Co.	2,849,028.95	
		10,346,798.83
MISCELLANEOUS INVESTMENTS ..		330,955.85
CASH WITH TRUSTEE OF SINKING FUND		10,082.77
CURRENT ASSETS—		
Inventory of Material, Supplies and Finished Goods	1,833,760.96	
Accounts and Bills Receivable ..	710,398.89	
U.S. Liberty Bonds	1,627.70	
Cash on Hand and in Banks ..	412,025.15	
		2,957,812.70
DEFERRED CHARGES		162,581.92
		$13,808,233.07

CONSOLIDATED INCOME ACCOUNT.
YEAR ENDING 31ST DECEMBER 1921.

Surplus Total at 1st January 1921 ..		$2,014,520.04
Less Dividends paid on Preferred Stock		78,964.00
		$1,935,556.04
Total Loss after deducting cost of operations including repairs and maintenance and upkeep, expenses of sales and general offices, doubtful accounts and adjustments of inventories, &c. ..	$791,425.07	
Add provision for interest, taxes, depreciation and depletion	345,485.97	
		1,136,911.04
Surplus as at 31st December 1921 ..		$798,645.00

TION and Subsidiary Corporations.
INCOME ACCOUNT, 31st December 1921.

Liabilities.

Capital Stock
Iron Products Corporation :
Preferred :
Authorised—30,000 Shares of $100. each $3,000,000.00

Outstanding—9,873 Shares of $100. each 987,300.00
Common of no par value :
Authorised—150,000 Shares
Outstanding—107,531 Shares 7,843,297.45
$8,830,597.45

Bonds and Mortgages of Subsidiaries		1,949,400.00
Accounts and Bills Payable ..		1,848,998.22
Reserves for Accrued Interest and Taxes, and for Accidents, Contingencies, &c.		380,592.40
Surplus of Subsidiaries when and as acquired	1,195,865.68	
Surplus earned since and adjusted as at 1st January 1921	818,654.36	
Surplus Total at 1st January 1921	2,014,520.04	
Loss for year ending 31st December 1921	1,136,911.04	
	877,609.00	
Less Dividends on Iron Products Corp. Preferred Stock ..	78,964.00	
		798,645.00
F. D. Griffiths, *Assistant Treasurer.*		$13,808,233.07

New York,
5th April 1922.

To the Directors,
Iron Products Corporation.

We have examined the books of Iron Products Corporation and its subsidiary owned and controlled corporations as at 31st December 1921.

The property accounts are stated at the amounts at which they appear on the books of the respective subsidiaries, except that patents and goodwill carried on the books at $6,144,194.58 are for balance sheet purposes stated at the nominal sum of one dollar ($1.00).

The inventories were valued at cost or market, whichever was lower, and have been accepted as recorded on the books.

The cash and securities on hand have been verified by actual inspection or by certificates from the depositories.

Subject to the foregoing we certify that in our opinion the attached balance sheet and income account show the true condition of the corporation at 31st December 1921.

E. E. Rossmore & Co., Inc.,
By E. E. Rossmore, C.P.A., *President.*

UNITED STATES
CONSOLIDATED GENERAL

Assets.

PROPERTY ACCOUNTS :			
Properties owned and operated by the several Companies—Balance of this account as of 31st December 1922, *less* Depletion and Depreciation Reserves			$1,631,579,206.38
ADVANCED MINING ROYALTIES :			
Payments for Advanced Mining Royalties	$32,579,830.41		
Less Reserved from Surplus to cover possible failure to realise all of the foregoing..	7,000,000.00		
		25,579,830.41	
MINING ROYALTIES—In respect of which non-interest bearing notes of the subsidiary companies have been issued. (See Contra)		31,612,507.22	
DEFERRED CHARGES (applying to future operations of the properties)			
Mine exploration expenses and other charges	$2,009,985.11		
Discount on Subsidiary Companies' Bonds sold (Net) ..	1,115,523.90		
		3,125,509.01	
INVESTMENTS :			
Outside Real Estate and Investments in sundry securities, including Real Estate Mortgages	$5,588,326.16		
Employees' Land Sales Contracts and Mortgages under Home-owning Plan ..	8,143,005.59		
		13,731,331.75	
SINKING AND RESERVE FUND ASSETS :			
Cash resources held by Trustees Account of Bond Sinking Funds	$1,233,298.21		
(In addition Trustees hold $159,222,000 of redeemed bonds, which are not treated as an asset.)			
Contingent Fund and Miscellaneous Assets	13,241,518.07		
Insurance and Depreciation Fund Assets and purchased Bonds available for future Bond Sinking Fund requirements, viz. :			
Securities $125,876,888.84*			
Cash .. 2,847,993.22			
Carried forward $128,724,882.06		14,474,816.28	1,705,628,384.77

STEEL CORPORATION.
BALANCE SHEET, 31ST DECEMBER 1922.

LIABILITIES

CAPITAL STOCK OF UNITED STATES STEEL CORPORATION		
Common	$508,302,500.00	
Preferred	360,281,100.00	
		$868,583,600.00
CAPITAL STOCKS OF SUBSIDIARY COMPANIES NOT HELD BY UNITED STATES STEEL CORPORATION (Par value)		403,242.50
BONDED, MORTGAGE AND DEBENTURE DEBT OUTSTANDING:		
United States Steel Corporation 50 Year 5% Bonds	$210,862,000.00	
United States Steel Corporation 10-60 Year 5% Bonds	170,045,000.00	
	$380,907,000.00	
Subsidiary Companies' Bonds, guaranteed by U.S. Steel Corporation	104,364,000.00	
Subsidiary Companies' Bonds, not guaranteed by U.S. Steel Corporation	54,311,061.24	
Subsidiary Companies' Real Estate Mortgages	158,206.50	
		539,740,267.74
SUBSIDIARY COMPANIES' NON-INTEREST BEARING NOTES —Maturing over a period of 35 years, substituted for previously existing mining royalty obligations—Guaranteed by United States Steel Corporation (See Contra)		31,612,507.22
CURRENT LIABILITIES:		
Current Accounts Payable and Pay Rolls	52,481,183.97	
Accrued Taxes, not yet due, including reserve for Federal Income Tax	26,077,842.66	
Accrued Interest, Unpresented Coupons and Unclaimed Dividends	7,535,856.57	
Preferred Stock Dividend No. 87, payable 27th February 1923	6,304,919.25	
Common Stock Dividend No. 74, payable 30th March 1923	6,353,781.25	
		98,753,583.70
Total Capital and Current Liabilities		1,539,093,201.16
	Carried forward	$1,539,093,201.16

United States Steel

Brought forward	128,724,882.06	14,474,816.28	1,705,628,384.77
Less Amount of foregoing investment represented by Capital Obligations of Subsidiary Companies not included as Liabilities in this Consolidated Balance Sheet..	20,377,421.00	108,347,461.06	122,822,277.31

CURRENT ASSETS :
Inventories, *less* Credit for Reserve and for amount of inventory values representing Profits earned by Subsidiary Companies on Inter-Company sales of products on hand in Inventories, 31st December 1922. (See Note)	$220,707,251.06	
Accounts Receivable ..	87,230,932.44	
Bills Receivable	6,978,010.35	
Agents' Balances	1,475,433.06	
Sundry Marketable Securities (including part of U.S. Government Securities owned)	59,605,056.45	
Time and other special Bank Deposits	9,505,739.26	
Cash (in Hand and on Deposit with Banks, Bankers and Trust Companies, subject to cheque)	126,700,131.69	
		512,202,554.31
		$2,340,653,216.42

*Includes $75,000,000 (par) of U.S. Liberty Loan Bonds reported in previous year's Balance Sheet under " Current Assets " in Sundry Marketable Securities.

We have audited the above Balance Sheet and certify that in our the United States Steel Corporation and Subsidiary Companies on

New York, 10*th March* 1923.

Here follows a Report setting out details of

Corporation.—(Contd.)

	Brought forward	1,539,093,201.16

SUNDRY RESERVES:
  Contingent, Miscellaneous Operating and other Reserves $133,337,457.02
  Insurance Reserves 28,184,229.28

  161,521,686.30

APPROPRIATED SURPLUS TO COVER CAPITAL EXPENDITURES:
  Invested in Property Account—Additions and Construction 140,898,914.10

UNDIVIDED SURPLUS OF UNITED STATES STEEL CORPORATION AND SUBSIDIARY COMPANIES:
  Capital Surplus provided in organisation $25,000,000.00
  Balance of Surplus accumulated by all companies from 1st April 1901 to 31st December 1922 .. .. .. 474,139,414.86

  Total, exclusive of Profits earned by Subsidiary Companies on Inter-Company Sales of Products on Hand in Inventories 31st December 1922 (see note below) 499,139,414.86

$2,340,653,216.42

NOTE.—That part of the surplus of Subsidiary Companies representing Profits accrued on sales of materials and products to other subsidiary companies and on hand in latters' Inventories is, in this Balance Sheet, deducted from the amount of Inventories included under Current Assets.

opinion it is properly drawn up so as to show the financial position of 31st December 1922.

PRICE, WATERHOUSE & CO.,
Auditors.

the figures in the above Balance Sheet.

UNITED STATES STEEL CORPORA
CONSOLIDATED INCOME ACCOUNT FOR

The total earnings were, after deducting all expenses incident to operations, including ordinary repairs and maintenance (approximately $88,000,000) and taxes (including reserve for Federal income-taxes), per General Profit and Loss Account		$109,788,916.32	
Less Interest on outstanding bonds and mortgages of the Subsidiary Companies		8,259,605.93	
Balance of Earnings in the year 1922		$101,529,310.39	
Less Charges and Allowances for Depletion and Depreciation applied as follows, viz. :—			
To Depreciation and Replacement Reserves and Sinking Funds on Bonds of Subsidiary Companies	$33,382,624.09		
To Sinking Funds on Bonds of U.S. Steel Corporation	9,305,884.70		
		42,688,508.79	
Net income in the year 1922		$58,840,801.60	
Deduct :			
Interest on U.S. Steel Corporation Bonds outstanding, viz. :—			
Fifty Year 5 per cent. Gold Bonds	$10,698,238.20		
Ten-Sixty Year 5 per cent. Gold Bonds	8,534,066.67		
	$19,232,304.87		
Premium paid on Bonds redeemed, viz. :			
On Subsidiary Companies' Bonds $150,205.98			
On U.S. Steel Corporation Bonds 724,873.04			
	875,079.02		
		20,107,383.89	
		$38,733,417.71	
Add Net Balance of sundry receipts and charges, including adjustments of various accounts		920,037.52	
Balance		$39,653,455.23	
Dividends for the year 1922 on U.S. Steel Corporation Stocks, viz. :			
Preferred :			
No. 84, 1¾ per cent., paid 29th May 1922	$6,304,919.25		
No. 85, 1¾ per cent., paid 30th August 1922	6,304,919.25		
No. 86, 1¾ per cent., paid 29th November 1922	6,304,919.25		
No. 87, 1¾ per cent., payable 27th Feb. 1923	6,304,919.25		
		$25,219,677.00	
Carried forward		$25,219,677.00	$39,653,455.23

TION AND SUBSIDIARY COMPANIES.
THE FISCAL YEAR ENDING 31ST DECEMBER 1922.

		Brought forward	$25,219,677.00	$39,653,455.23
Common :				
No. 71, 1¼ per cent., paid 29th June 1922	$6,353,781.25			
No. 72, 1¼ per cent., paid 29th September 1922	6,353,781.25			
No. 73, 1¼ per cent., paid 30th December 1922	6,353,781.25			
No. 74, 1¼ per cent., payable 30th March 1923	6,353,781.25			
			25,415,125.00	
				50,634,802.00
Balance provided from Undivided Surplus				$10,981,346.77
Undivided Surplus on 31st December 1921		$483,926,957.59		
Add Adjustments..		1,193,804.04		
				485,120,761.63

Total Undivided Surplus 31st December 1922, exclusive of capital surplus provided in organisation and of Subsidiary Companies' Inter-Company Profits in Inventories $474,139,414.86

We certify that in our opinion the above Income Account is a fair and correct statement of the Earnings and Income of the United States Steel Corporation and Subsidiary Companies for the fiscal year ending 31st December 1922.

PRICE, WATERHOUSE & CO.,

New York, 10*th March* 1923.   *Auditors.*

United States Steel Corporation
PROPERTY INVESTMENT

Gross Fixed Property Investment Account, 31st December 1921, exclusive of Stripping and Mine Development, Structural Erection and Logging Plants, per Annual Report	$2,038,576,260.40	
Sundry adjustments during 1922 in the foregoing balance	1,636,167.31	
		$2,040,212,427.71
Capital Expenditures on Property Account in 1922	$26,844,307.54	
Less—Amount written off to Depreciation and Replacement Reserves for investment cost of improvements and equipment dismantled and retired	6,019,670.94	
		20,824,636.60
		$2,061,037,064.31
Less — Property values written off to Depletion Reserves		6,399.76
Gross Fixed Property Investment Account, 31st December 1922		$2,061,030,664.55
Less—Depreciation and Depletion Reserves, 31st December 1922:		
Balances in various Reserve Accounts	$307,191,303.88	
Specifically applied for redemption of bonds through Bond Sinking Funds	154,406,430.65	
		461,597,734.53
Net Fixed Property Investment Account, 31st December 1922		$1,599,432,930.02
	Carried forward	$1,599,432,930.02

and Subsidiary Companies.— (Contd.)
ACCOUNTS 31ST DECEMBER 1922.

		Brought forward	$1,599,432,930.02
Investment in Stripping and Development at Mines and in Structural Erection and Logging Plants, viz. :			
Balance at 31st December 1921		$29,418,921.06	
Expended during the year 1922	$5,966,400.43		
Less— Charged off in 1922 to operating expenses	3,239,045.13		
Net Increase in the year 1922		2,727,355.30	
			32,146,276.36
Total of Property Investment Account, 31st December 1922, per Consolidated General Balance Sheet			$1,631,579,206.38

APPROPRIATED SURPLUS TO COVER CAPITAL EXPENDITURE, 31ST DECEMBER 1922.

Amount of appropriations made from Surplus Net Income prior to 1st January 1908, applied in payment of capital expenditures, and in the Consolidated General Balance Sheet formally written off to credit of the Property Investment Account	$162,795,509.45
Amount of appropriations made from Surplus Net Income since 1st January 1908, applied in payment of same class of expenditures, but in the Consolidated General Balance Sheet carried in the account " Appropriated Surplus to cover Capital Expenditures "	140,898,914.10
Total	$303,694,423.55

United States Steel Corporation
CONDENSED GENERAL PROFIT

GROSS RECEIPTS—Gross Sales and Earnings		$1,092,697,772.36
OPERATING CHARGES, VIZ.:		
Manufacturing and Producing Cost and Operating Expenses, including ordinary maintenance and repairs and provisional charges by subsidiary companies for depreciation	$959,973,966.88	
Administrative, Selling and General Expenses (not including general expenses of transportation companies)	30,331,295.78	
Taxes (including reserve for Federal income taxes)	35,798,449.97	
Commercial Discounts and Interest	6,854,030.13	
	$1,032,957,742.76	
Less—Amount included in above charges for allowances for depletion and depreciation here deducted for purpose of showing same in separate item of charge, as see below	33,382,624.09	999,575,118.67
Balance		$93,122,653.69
Sundry Net Manufacturing and Operating Gains and Losses, including idle plant expenses, royalties received, &c.	£3,232,606.13	
Rentals Received	921,564.67	4,154,170.80
Total Net Manufacturing, Producing and Operating Income before deducting provisional charges for depreciation		97,276,824.49
	Carried forward	$97,276,824.49

and Subsidiary Companies.—(Contd.)
AND LOSS ACCOUNT, 31ST DECEMBER, 1922.

	Brought forward	$97,276,824.49
OTHER INCOME AND CHARGES.		
Net Profits of properties owned, but whose operations (gross revenue, cost of product, expenses, &c.) are not classified in this statement	$198,569.72	
Income from sundry investments and interest on deposits, &c.	13,493,163.37	
		13,691,733.09
Balance		$110,968,557.58
Less—Net Balance of Profits earned by subsidiary companies on sales made and service rendered account of materials on hand at close of year in purchsing companies' inventories and which profits have not yet been realised in cash from the standpoint of a combined statement of the business of all companies		1,179,641.26
Total Earnings in the year 1922, per Income Account		$109,788,916.32
Less—Interest Charges on Subsidiary Companies' Bonds and Mortgages		8,259,605.93
Balance of Earnings for the year before deducting provisional charges for depreciation		$101,529,310.39
Less, Charges and Allowances for Depletion and Depreciation, viz. :		
By Subsidiary Companies	$33,382,624.09	
By U.S. Steel Corporation	9,305,884.70	
		42,688,508.79
Net Income in the year 1922		$58,840,801.60

CERTIFICATE OF INDEPENDENT AUDITORS.

New York, 10th March 1923.

To the Stockholders of the United States Steel Corporation.

We have examined the books of the United States Steel Corporation and Subsidiary Companies for the year ending 31st December 1922, and certify that the Balance Sheet at that date and the relative income account are correctly prepared therefrom.

The charges to property account during the year cover only actual additions and extensions to the properties and plants, and the provision made for depletion and depreciation is, in our opinion, fair and reasonable. The item of deferred charges represents expenditures reasonably and properly carried forward to operations in subsequent years.

The valuations of the stocks of materials and supplies on hand, as shown by inventories certified by the responsible officials, have been carefully made at prices not in excess of cost or market, and, as stated in the directors' report, a substantial reserve has been deducted from the values so determined. Full provision has been made for bad and doubtful accounts receivable and for all ascertainable liabilities.

We have verified the cash and securities by actual inspection or by certificates from the depositaries, and are of opinion that the marketable bonds and stocks included in current assets are worth the value at which they are stated in the Balance Sheet, and

WE CERTIFY that, in our opinion, the Balance Sheet is properly drawn up so as to show the financial position of the Corporation and Subsidiary Companies on 31st December 1922, and the relative income account is a fair and correct statement of the net earnings for the fiscal year ending at that date.

PRICE, WATERHOUSE & CO.

INSTITUTE OF CHARTERED ACCOUNTANTS IN ENGLAND AND WALES.

PROCEEDINGS OF THE AUTUMNAL MEETING

HELD AT BIRMINGHAM,
on 11th, 12th and 13th
October, 1928.

LONDON :
PUBLISHED BY AUTHORITY OF THE COUNCIL OF THE INSTITUTE
BY GEE & CO. (PUBLISHERS) LTD., 6 KIRBY STREET, E.C.1.
1928.

TABLE OF CONTENTS

	PAGE
MEETING	5
CIVIC RECEPTION	12
PRESIDENTIAL ADDRESS	17
LUNCHEON BY BIRMINGHAM SOCIETY	33
VISIT TO THE BOTANICAL GARDENS	34
A PAPER: "Limitations of a Balance Sheet," by SIR GILBERT GARNSEY, K.B.E., F.C.A.	35
THE LORD MAYOR'S RECEPTION	59
A PAPER: "If I were the Chancellor, or Budgetary Finance," by H. LAKIN-SMITH, F.C.A.	60
VISITS TO MANUFACTORIES	86
THE CONFERENCE BANQUET	86
A VISIT TO SHAKESPEARE'S COUNTRY	104
GOLF COMPETITION	106

AFTERNOON SESSION

The afternoon session was held in the Temperance Hall, Temple Street, and was well attended.

The President of the Institute occupied the chair, and in opening the meeting said that although it was his pleasure to introduce to them Sir Gilbert Garnsey, it was not really necessary as he was probably known to most of them, and they all knew his writings. He did not quite know why they had moved to the Temperance Hall, unless it was because the remarks of Sir Gilbert Garnsey were going to be so far from dry that it needed something to neutralise the effect of them. (Laughter.)

Sir Gilbert Garnsey, K.B.E., F.C.A., then read the following paper :—

Limitations of a Balance Sheet
PRELIMINARY

IN recent years a growing volume of criticism of the published balance sheets of some of our public companies indicates that not only shareholders but many other interested parties feel that in some cases they are not obtaining information to which they consider they are entitled. I say "in some cases" because, so far as I can gather, the criticism is in the main levelled at the few.

From some of the comments which appear from time to time it seems clear, however, that such information as is given is often misunderstood or not fully appreciated, and as a result the criticism which follows it is not always well directed.

The sources of criticism are very widespread and include shareholders, bankers, creditors, stock-brokers, the financial Press, economists, financiers and speculators. Each of these groups is looking to the same document, viz., the balance sheet, supplemented in some cases by a Profit and Loss Account, to provide the information of particular interest to themselves.

The following examples will serve to illustrate the nature of the demands for information : (a) the fact that many reconstructions have taken place in companies whose balance sheets have given little or no indication that the assets proposed to be written down (almost invariably the capital assets) were overstated ; (b) no indication of the break-up value of the assets in the event of liquidation and forced sales ; (*c*) the grouping together under " omnibus " headings of assets or liabilities of very different types ; (*d*) lack of information as to the value of investments in subsidiary companies ; (*e*) concealment of reserves by undervaluation of assets or over-statement of liabilities ; (*f*) insufficient information as to the nature of the profits ; (*g*) the impossibility of valuing the shares of a company from its published accounts, and (*h*) the lack of a standardised form which makes statistical comparisons between companies and trades impossible ; even the same company does not always present its accounts in the same form.

These examples serve to illustrate the variety of the points of view from which a balance sheet is regarded.

Whilst some of the demands for fuller information seem quite justifiable it would appear that some critics are not quite clear as to what information they ought to have, or to what use they could put it if they had it. This is not surprising when it is remembered that the enormous growth of joint stock companies during the last fifty years has transferred the ownership of industrial capital from the hands of a comparatively few business men who were experts in their own particular trade, to a vast number of investors who have little, if any, knowledge of the technical side of the businesses in which they have invested. Methods of presentation of accounts which were adequate for the consideration of persons who were familiar with the detailed operations of the business, may not provide sufficient information for thousands of investors who are not familiar with that particular business, or possibly with any business.

Many of those who are charged with the duty of presenting accounts, while admitting the truth of this contention, realise that a solution satisfactory to all interested parties is by no means simple, and in many cases is not possible.

It is proposed to consider here the main purpose of a balance sheet, in what manner it should be presented in order best to effect that purpose, and what are the limitations which must be recognised before useful inferences can be drawn from a study of the figures.

The Main Purpose of a Balance Sheet

A Balance Sheet and Profit and Loss Account represent primarily an accounting by the executive to the proprietors. They are in fact historical records which should be regarded as part of a series from which the general trend of the business may be inferred.

The balance sheet purports to show the position at a particular moment only, indicating how the resources of the company are employed at that moment and from that point of view may be compared to an instantaneous photograph. The actual position may, of course, vary from day to day.

The Profit and Loss Account on the other hand, is not a stationary picture, but should show the course of affairs through a period of time. In some businesses it is probably of more importance than the balance sheet, both in estimating the present worth and the future potentialities of the concern.

In deciding upon the best form in which accounts should be presented, the interests of shareholders should come first, and as a general rule this consideration is given full weight. Other interests should be satisfied only in so far as they do not conflict with those of the shareholders. It is by no means always simple to decide what are the best interests of shareholders in a particular case, and it should not be assumed that the problem could be solved by legislation or by the voluntary adoption of general rules. There will always be exceptional cases which must each be judged on its own merits, and it is frequently the exceptional cases which meet with most criticism.

No doubt by now it is generally known by the investing public, but it will bear re-statement, that the form of the published accounts and the information given therein are matters for the directors of a company to decide, and not for the auditors. Naturally if the auditors form the opinion that the statements proposed to be published do not give a correct view of the state of the company's affairs, then they would have a great deal to say about it before appending their report.

Auditors are, in fact, frequently consulted by directors when settling the form or deciding what information is to be given, and I have no doubt that their advice is in the direction of giving as much information as the directors feel they are able to do without incurring undue risk to the business, having regard to all the circumstances.

After all, it is impracticable to make Balance Sheets and Profit and Loss Accounts completely informative for, of necessity, they must be summarised to make them suitable for publication.

I think it will be admitted that in the majority of cases the published accounts of public companies in this country are straightforward, honest statements, and give shareholders as much information as can reasonably be condensed into summary form.

It is as well, however, to recognise that under modern complex conditions the affairs of a large company cannot always be properly comprehended from a single condensed statement; indeed, it is hardly possible in one statement to meet all the demands for information. Where this is the case a balance sheet might well be, and indeed sometimes is, supplemented by a series of financial statements. This course is followed by some of the large American industrial companies, and it might well be that along these lines some further progress is possible. In many cases such statements can be prepared by anyone interested from a series of published Balance Sheet and Profit and Loss Accounts.

Information Required by an Investor

Before discussing the accounts in detail it may be useful to decide what is the information required, say, by a shareholder to enable him to estimate the value of his investment and then to see to what extent the required information can be obtained from the accounts.

It is perhaps as well to mention in parenthesis that probably two of the most important factors in connection with any business are the quality of the management, and what so often follows from it, the goodwill or maybe the lack of co-operation of the employees. Few businesses run themselves, and the success or failure of any particular company is often largely dependent on the men who are running it. The manner in which accounts are presented may, no doubt, at times throw some light on the character of those in control, but it is, of course, impossible to include in a balance sheet, or indeed to measure in any way the value, if any, attaching to a business in respect of these two factors, through the consequences of good or bad management and the co-operation or otherwise of the employees is often reflected in the financial position and in the profit and loss figures from time to time.

Apart from the management, probably the important questions from the point of view of the actual or prospective investor are: (a) What is the probable future earning capacity

LIMITATIONS OF A BALANCE SHEET

of the company? (*b*) How are profits likely to be dealt with? (*c*) Is the business immediately solvent or, put in another way, is the working capital (that is, the excess of current assets over current liabilities) adequate for the immediate purposes of the company? (*d*) Is the business over-capitalised from the point of view of its issued capital, or is it under-capitalised (i.e. is the capital insufficient for the company's needs)?

As to (*a*), that is, earning capacity, this is referred to later.

In considering (*b*), that is, the probable use that will be made of profits, this can, as a rule, only be inferred from an examination of a series of past balance sheets and reports from which past policy can be gathered. The retention of a considerable portion of the profits in the business may affect the immediate value of a company's shares, but if the profits are real and are used judiciously, appreciation in value of the shares will only be a question of time.

With regard to (*c*), the balance sheet usually shows whether the current assets exceed the current liabilities which, taken into account with present commitments, will indicate whether the business has adequate working capital for its needs. While profits are maintained at a high level, this may not be a vital point, as it will usually not be difficult to arrange finance under such conditions, but a deficiency of current assets is generally undesirable except as a purely temporary expedient as an unforeseen lean period might bring unfortunate results.

As to (*d*), over capitalisation can best be tested by reference to the earning capacity of a business. Provided that the net profits, after making provision for all prior charges, are sufficient to ensure a reasonable return on the issued capital, having regard to the nature of the business and the risks involved, then it can hardly be said that a company is suffering from over-capitalisation. In the case of new undertakings where there is no past record of earnings, this test cannot be applied, and it is only possible to see that the issued capital does not exceed the present estimated value of the net assets, including a reasonable figure for any goodwill, patent rights, &c., which may have been acquired. In both cases the position should be capable of ascertainment from the published accounts.

Under-capitalisation (by which it is not intended to imply the converse of over-capitalisation) is usually evidenced by an undue proportion of borrowed money or of trade creditors: this is sometimes a gradual process, which may be brought about by a continuous expenditure on capital assets in excess of the profits retained in the business, or by an expansion of business requiring the carrying of larger stocks, and possibly a greater volume of outstanding debtors, than was contemplated when the original capital was fixed. The importance to the shareholder of such a state of affairs is that it cannot be regarded as permanent, and it may lead to the raising of further permanent capital on terms which may or may not be advantageous to existing shareholders.

It will be seen that the answer to the last two questions is largely dependent upon the basis upon which the various assets have been valued in the published accounts. We therefore come to the question of valuation.

BALANCE SHEET VALUES

The basis upon which the various assets are valued will depend to some extent on the nature of the business and the objects for which the company was formed. In this connection it is well to bear in mind that a balance sheet is not a statement of affairs as that term is understood in liquidation procedure; that is to say, it is not intended to show the estimated realisable value of the assets if they were offered for sale.

It is a statement drawn up in respect of a going concern, and should show the position as a going concern.

Broadly speaking, the assets of a company will fall into two main categories: (*i*) *fixed or capital assets*, i.e. those assets which are not held for the purpose of re-sale, but the possession of which is essential to enable the company to carry on its business, and (*ii*) *floating or current assets*, i.e. cash, debtors or stocks held for the sole purpose of conversion into cash at a profit. Between these two categories no definite line can be drawn applicable to all cases: they will vary in different businesses and in the same business at different times, but there should be no difficulty in making the classification in any particular case.

There are other items which often appear on the assets of a balance sheet consisting of amounts unrepresented by any tangible assets, such as preliminary and other expenditure being written off against profits over a term of years, losses and so on, but as these are usually shown as separate items in the accounts (and must be under the new Companies Act) it is not proposed to discuss them here.

The division between assets and current assets is very necessary and very important, as balance sheets do not as a rule purport to show the realisable value of the fixed assets (whether as a going concern or as the amount which might be realised by a sale), while, on the other hand, it may be taken for granted, unless otherwise stated, that the current assets are shown at figures not in excess of their realisable value.

Capital assets are, in fact, stated at conventional or token values, while current assets are shown not in excess of real values.

Fixed or Capital Assets.

Every balance sheet should state the basis upon which the values of the fixed or capital assets have been arrived at, as unless this is known any deductions drawn from the figures may be misleading. In this connection it should be noted that the new Companies Act makes it necessary for a public company to distinguish in every balance sheet between the amounts of its fixed and floating assets and must state how the values of the fixed assets have been arrived at. I regard this change in the law as of very considerable importance, and it should be found of great assistance to shareholders and others interested in the financial affairs of a company.

The capital assets of a manufacturing concern will consist of such items as goodwill, patent rights, land, buildings, plant, machinery, loose tools and so on, including possibly holdings in subsidiary companies. It is against these assets that the weight of criticism is most often directed and in so far as objection is taken to the grouping of the items, it is frequently justified.

In many cases it may be of value to know the nature and amounts of the individual capital assets, the additional expenditure each year and the amount of depreciation, if any, provided for are also important and should be considered in conjunction with the resources of the company and its earning capacity. In a large number of cases sufficient information is generally given, but it must be admitted that some balance sheets are not very informative in this direction.

It is, however, on the question of values that most of the criticism arises. In the case of unsuccessful companies which go into liquidation, the capital assets rarely realise a figure approaching their book values and in these circumstances many shareholders appear to feel that they have a grievance against those responsible for the balance sheets.

It is difficult, however, to see in what way a shareholder would benefit by the inclusion in the balance sheet of a going concern of an estimate of the break-up value of the capital assets, an estimate which actual realisation, if found to be necessary, might prove to be very wide of the mark.

Such estimates would naturally vary from year to year according to conditions, and would only be of real value when liquidation was in sight. The cases in which an investor would be well advised to invest in the hopes of a profit on liquidation are very few, and already existing shareholders could hardly benefit from the publication of an estimate of the proceeds of liquidation which would of necessity be on a conservative basis.

It is the common practice to set out the capital assets in a balance sheet at their cost, usually less deductions for depreciation due to age, use or obsolescence, and it should not be assumed that the balance sheet figures necessarily reflect the fair present value in use or for sale of such capital assets.

As to such assets as plant and machinery, it is true that their value may not be properly measured by including them at actual cost less depreciation; neither is the value to be found necessarily in the cost of replacement at the present time. The value may greatly exceed replacement cost if, for example, immediate profit earning opportunities are exceptional; or it may be very much less if, for instance, an equally effective plant of an entirely different type could be set up at a much smaller cost, or again if the plant cannot be worked at a profit, its value may not exceed scrap.

Within these very wide limits the value at any particular time will depend on earning capacity, and as this fluctuates, the maximum and minimum value will be fixed by first one and then another of the factors mentioned.

If it appears that the value of the capital assets, based upon their earning capacity, has permanently fallen much below the balance sheet figures so that there is no prospect of earning an economic return on the nominal value of the share capital, then it may be decided to reconstruct by reducing the capital and writing down the capital assets to a figure more in accord with their earning capacity. Such a step would be foreshadowed by the diminishing profits. The balance sheet figures do not indicate year by year that there is a specific reduction in the value of the fixed assets, for it will be readily appreciated that it is not practicable to calculate each year and include in a balance sheet the value of a large plant on any such complex basis. Even if it were done, it would not appear to add any useful information in estimating the value of a business as a going concern. The annual fluctuations would have no definite significance and the average investor would probably be more mystified than at present.

The advantages of the basis of costless depreciation are undeniable when the problem is approached from this point of view. It is the only basis on which it is possible to compile a continuous historical record as the annual changes do possess a definite significance and should be studied in conjunction with the changes in the resources of the company.

It is true that with certain special companies (e.g. investment trust companies) capital assets are in some cases valued annually by the directors, and in other cases (e.g. at the formation of a new company) by expert valuers called in for the purpose, but these are, however, exceptional cases, and no general rule can be drawn from them.

Bearing in mind that the sale of its capital assets is not contemplated by a going concern, it would appear that the conventional method of stating these at cost less depreciation is more useful than any alternative method.

On the question of the provision for depreciation or accruing renewals, the Courts appear to have held that under certain circumstances a company is not bound to provide out of its profits for any depreciation of its capital assets before paying dividends; nevertheless, it is customary for all soundly managed concerns to do so, for the very good reason that, unless a fund to meet depreciation or replacement of wasting or obsolescent assets is provided from other sources, the company will eventually be unable to carry on business. The published accounts should, and in fact usually do, indicate whether any such provision is being made.

Investments in Subsidiary Companies.

With regard to investments or holdings in subsidiary companies, I have already written* at some length on this somewhat difficult question, and to-day I can only refer very briefly to some of the more important points which arise in connection therewith.

"*Holding Companies and their Accounts," published by Gee & Co., (Publishers), Ltd.

The actual cost of the shares acquired is probably the basis most frequently used for inclusion in the balance sheet. It must be assumed that at the time of the purchase the directors of the holding company considered the shares worth the price paid, and a balance sheet of the holding company prepared immediately after the purchase should properly include that investment at cost. It is possible that a valuation on some other basis (e.g. market value or earning capacity) would, in certain cases, give a different figure, especially, for example, where the holding company is itself a manufacturing company and acquired the shares of a competitive concern : in such a case benefits might be expected to accrue to the holding company which would be worth paying for though they would never be reflected in the figures of the subsidiary company itself.

Cost therefore appears to be a sound basis as a starting point, but adjustments will probably have to be made from time to time to give effect to reductions in the capital value of the investments, which may arise in various ways. For example, at the date of the acquisition of the shares the subsidiary company may have undivided profits and reserves which are available for distribution, and which have been taken into account in fixing the price to be paid for the shares by the holding company. The assets constituting these undivided profits and reserves, therefore, form a part of the total net assets representing the capital invested by the holding company in the subsidiary, and any dividend paid by the subsidiary to the holding company out of those profits which existed at the date of the acquisition of the shares would in fact represent a return of capital to the holding company and should be so treated by deducting the amount from the cost of the investment. Again, if the subsidiary company has incurred a net trading loss since the shares were acquired, the assets have been depleted to that extent and the holding company, should meet this position by setting aside an equivalent sum out of its own profits; this amount would represent a reduction in the cost of the investment.

A similar position would arise if the exchange value of the shares of the subsidiary company had been fixed by reference to a valuation of its assets in excess of their book values. It might be that the subsidiary company would distribute its profits as dividend without making any provision for the additional depreciation calculated on the increased values. In order that the holding company may keep its own capital intact it should make provision out of its own profits for the additional depreciation and at the same time reduce the original figure representing the cost of the investment. Other adjustments of a similar character will occur in practice, but these examples serve as illustrations.

So far as the published balance sheet is concerned, the best method would appear to be to include investments in subsidiary companies at cost price, subject to adjustments such as those already mentioned, and to supplement this where practicable with either a consolidated balance sheet, showing the combined position of the whole group, or a statement showing the combined assets and liabilities of the subsidiary companies which make up the capital invested in those concerns.

The new Companies Act contains some provisions with regard to information to be given in the balance sheets of holding companies, to which I refer later.

Floating or Current Assets.

The current assets should be set out separately in the balance sheet and not combined with the capital assets, and in a similar way the current liabilities should be distinguished from capital and long-dated indebtedness. This is the usual practice, and a summary can readily be made to show whether there is a surplus or deficiency, that is to say, whether the business from that point of view is in a good or bad financial position. Bankers would prepare such a summary before making advances, and would usually ascertain how previous resources had been disposed of, whether arising from capital issues, loans, or profits retained in the business.

Similar statements would be useful to shareholders and others and can usually be prepared from a series of consecutive balance sheets.

The methods of valuation of the current assets always receives the most careful attention of the auditor and he particularly directs his attention to see that they are not included at a figure in excess of their realisable value to a going concern.

The methods of valuation employed for such current assets as stocks are of great importance, when it is remembered that the sole purpose for which the company holds these assets is to endeavour to convert them into cash at a profit, and the value at which they are brought into the accounts will affect the amount of profit shown.

The general principle is that no profit should be taken into the accounts in respect of any unsold products, that is to say, a rise in value unaccompanied by a sale should not normally be regarded as profit; nevertheless it is customary, and the custom is a prudent one, to make provision out of realised profits, for any loss which it is anticipated will be incurred by the subsequent sale of products unsold at the date of the balance sheet.

This procedure is usually carried out by valuing work in progress and stocks on hand at cost or market value, whichever is the lower. Debtors are included at their net estimated realisable value, after making provision for bad and doubtful debts, if any, and so on.

Here, again, it is necessary to point out that an estimate of the amount which might be realised in the event of a liquidation by, say, a forced sale of unsold products could be of little practical value to the investor in a going concern.

Liabilities.

A reference should perhaps be made to the liabilities of a company. All liabilities which are known as having accrued at the date of the account, with the addition of a due proportion of accruing liabilities, are included in the balance sheet, as well as a note of any contingent liabilities which may directly or indirectly affect the financial position of the company.

Current liabilities should be distinguished from capital and long-dated indebtedness, and it is important that liabilities which are secured on any of the assets of the company should be separately stated. It is as well to note that when the new Act comes into force secured liabilities must be so described, thus confirming the best practice at the present time.

Secret Reserves.

Some reference is also called for here to the question of " Secret " Reserves, as it not infrequently happens that reserves of this character are included in the balance sheet along with the item sundry creditors under some comprehensive heading, though the exact amount is generally known only to the directors and officials of the company.

Secret or internal reserves arise from a variety of circumstances, some of which are above criticism, but others have been the subject of much discussion amongst accountants, shareholders and others. They are usually created in times of exceptional prosperity, and, so long as they are made from prudent motives, the result is generally of advantage to shareholders.

"Secret" reserves may take various forms, such as the writing down to nominal figures of valuable capital assets, valuing stocks on hand below their true values, providing excessive depreciation, excessive reserves for bad debts, taxation and known contingencies, making special reserves for possible future contingencies, and so on.

It is common knowledge that most of the more prosperous concerns have some reserves of this character, and it should not be assumed that there is anything necessarily wrong in such a practice.

No exception can reasonably be taken to an undisclosed provision in advance for such contingencies as are incident to the nature of the business, more particularly in cases where the business is of a fluctuating character, or where its success is largely dependent on the maintenance of very high credit.

The sudden disclosure of special losses, or the publication of results which fluctuate considerably from time to time, may easily be inimical to the best interest of the shareholders by unduly depressing the market prices of their shares.

Directors exercise a wise discretion in protecting shareholders against any such contingencies by making ample provisions—when profits permit.

The argument usually advanced against such a course is that it involves an injustice to shareholders who sell without knowledge of the amount of the reserves. Such cases, however, are very rare. Apart from the fact that the Stock Exchange and shareholders generally pay little regard to the value of particular assets in fixing the price of the shares of a successful company (and it is generally the successful companies which have undisclosed reserves), it is usually assumed that such reserves do exist, only the amount being unknown. The price of the shares being normally fixed by the profits and dividends paid, the knowledge that some secret reserves exist would tend to increase the price. We are sometimes inclined to exaggerate what is known to exist but is unmeasured, and it is quite possible for this reason that in most cases a shareholder selling his shares receives at least as much as he would do if the amount of the reserve had been known to him.

As to what disclosure should be made by a company this must depend upon the circumstances of each case, though, obviously, publicity is always desirable if it involves no undue risk or injury to the best interests of the business and its shareholders. It is unwise to be dogmatic on this question and each case must be judged on its merits.

No doubt there are cases which call for criticism, but on the whole it cannot be said that the practice is abused, or that shareholders as a whole suffer in consequence.

Earning Capacity

It would not be disputed that earning capacity is a very important factor in determining the value of a business.

So far as it is possible to ascertain it from the accounts, the probable earning capacity can, as a rule, only be estimated with approximate accuracy if Profit and Loss Accounts covering a series of years are available, giving a reasonable amount of information as to the nature of the profits earned in each period.

In the case of most of the old-established companies, whose accounts extend over a number of years, it is usually possible to get a fairly accurate view of their earning capacity from the information disclosed in their published accounts, but this cannot be said of all businesses and with concerns of more recent growth; where only a few years' results are available, more detailed information is usually necessary before any very reliable estimate can be made.

Where it is possible to do so without undue risk, trading profits should be distinguished from special profits, whether arising in the period or not.

A certain amount of criticism has been directed against the lack of information provided in some cases in the published accounts as to the nature and volume of the profits earned in any specified period. Whilst the criticism may be merited in specific cases, it is not possible to lay down general rules governing the information that should always be supplied. Considerable difficulty is often experienced in attempting to decide what is best for the shareholders. In cases of severe competition, when one business is attempting to drive another out of existence, there might be considerable disadvantage in disclosing any details which would help the competitor in the struggle. Generally speaking, however, important competitors have other sources from which they can obtain more information about a business than is shown in the accounts.

In forming an opinion upon the prospective earning capacity of a company, besides the information which may be drawn from the accounts, it is of equal importance to know the character of the management, the probable conditions of demand for the company's products, the supply of raw materials, and so on, and it is of little use to blame the published accounts for a failure to foreshadow adverse conditions or to express these important factors.

Further, it should be borne in mind that though it is necessary in practice to allocate profits to definite periods of time, in many cases these profits are due to varied activities extending over much longer periods. In estimating an annual earning capacity, therefore, profits ought in theory to be attributed to the period over which they were being worked for and earned, and not to the particular period in which they become sufficiently accurately ascertained and assured to justify their being dealt with in the accounts as realised profits.

A further consideration is that industrial profits are usually earned by processes which involve the exhaustion of capital assets. Before the earning capacity can be measured, provision should be made to cover this exhaustion. It may be that no provision need be made before ascertaining the profit available for dividends; for example, if the plant has been previously written off entirely, but in such a case the future earning capacity of the business may be overstated if no such deduction is made.

Attention may be drawn here to a point which is frequently misunderstood regarding the effect on the accounts of a so-called conservative policy. The main burden of such a policy would fall upon the first year of its adoption; thereafter the effect would be limited to the growth in that element of the business to which the policy is being applied. For example, if stock were to be undervalued consistently, the profits will be understated in the first year, but not afterwards, unless the volume of stock is increasing; on the other hand, in a year in which the volume of stock is reduced the profits would be overstated.

Again, if the "conservative" policy were to take the form of charging annually against profits expenditure, say, of a capital nature, the time may come when the amounts so charged will be less than the depreciation which would have been provided had the expenditure been capitalised.

The point it is desired to draw attention to is that though a company may be known to be following a conservative policy, that does not necessarily imply that the profits for the current year are under-stated; in fact, the opposite may probably be true in the case of a formerly progressive business which is now beginning to decline. It is not intended to belittle the value of conservatism, but its effect on the accounts is not always appreciated.

Examples might be multiplied to illustrate the difference between the problems of estimating earning capacity to which the above is very relevant and ascertaining the profits for which credit may properly be taken in the accounts of a particular year. It is sufficient for the present purpose to emphasise the difference and to point out that a Profit and Loss Account should not necessarily be regarded as an attempt to show the earning capacity of the business but should rather be considered as part of a continuous historical record; there are instances, no doubt, where without analysis it would be unwise to regard it as reflecting more than the amount of profit which may fairly be regarded as having been earned up to date and which has not been taken up in the accounts of previous periods.

Nevertheless, the published accounts are usually the chief source of information for the investor, present or prospective, and this fact should be borne in mind by those responsible for their preparation. Consideration should therefore be given to the form adopted with a view to the avoidance where possible of anything which would mislead the investor in the inferences which he would be justified in drawing from them.

Conclusion

It is extremely important that shareholders and others should realise the limitations of even the best accounts; the shorter the period covered by the accounts, the greater are the limitations. It may be that too much is expected from balance sheets: in essence they are historical records and correct conclusions can hardly be drawn from a hurried survey of temporary conditions, but rather by a careful examination with the object of distinguishing between permanent tendencies and temporary fluctuations.

It must be understood that a balance sheet is usually a combination of real and conventional (usually cost) figures which in a complex business can only be understood after the most careful study and comparison with previous accounts. The values at which the capital assets are stated are usually, though not always, on the conventional basis of actual cost,less a deduction representing the estimated amount of exhaustion due to wear and tear, &c. The report of the auditors that the balance sheet shows " the true and correct view of the state of the company's affairs " should be read in this light. Auditors are not expert valuers for this purpose : they satisfy themselves that the amount stated to have been spent on capital assets has been so spent, but they must not be understood to express the opinion that the money has been well spent or that the capital assets are necessarily worth the figures stated.

In spite, however, of the many limitations which have been touched upon, balance sheets are nevertheless of very great value. It will be admitted, speaking quite generally, that there is room for some improvement in the form of many published accounts ; on the whole, the tendency is in the right direction, and the need for further information is being more readily met.

When the Companies Act, 1928, comes into force every public company must lay before its shareholders once a year a Balance Sheet and Profit and Loss Account. While there is no reference as to the details which are to be set out in the profit and loss account,the Act provides that every balance sheet must give such particulars as are necessary to disclose the general nature of the assets and the liabilities.

It must distinguish between the amounts respectively of the fixed and floating assets and must state how the values of the fixed assets have been arrived at ; any preliminary and other expenses in connection with issues of capital must be shown separately as well as the amounts of the goodwill and any patents and trade marks where it is possible to ascertain them. Any secured liability must be so described, though it will not be necessary to specify the assets on which the liability is secured.

Holding companies must set out the aggregate amount of shares in or amounts owing from subsidiary companies, distinguishing between shares and indebtedness and, similarly, the aggregate amount of indebtedness to subsidiary companies must be shown separately from the other liabilities. A statement must also be attached to the balance sheet showing how the aggregate profits and losses of subsidiary companies (so far as they concern the holding company) have been dealt with in the accounts of the holding company.

The annual accounts will also have to contain particulars of any loans to directors and officers of the company and show the total amounts paid to the directors (but not including managing directors) as remuneration whether by the company or any subsidiary company.

It will be seen that these alterations in the law are all in the direction of affording more information. It is true that many balance sheets already give these particulars, and the new legislation, when in force, will have the effect of standardising the best practice.

As has already been mentioned, the actual form in which accounts are presented is not the direct responsibility of the auditors, but there is an indirect obligation which is not regarded lightly.

Our profession is looked upon by many as the final arbiter in matters of account and rightly so; whilst, therefore, the auditor has no legal right to decide the form in which accounts shall be presented, he has a moral duty to endeavour to secure improvement where it seems possible.

It may be possible to lead where it would be impossible to drive and this would be made easier by a careful study of all points of view; it will often be found that objections to suggested alterations are not entirely without reason and a sympathetic study of the point of view of the objector may result in an alternative suggestion which meets both sides.

It might, perhaps, be noted here that of those critics interested in a balance sheet, the economists' point of view differs essentially from the others.

Shareholders, bankers, creditors, financiers, &c., all have a personal interest in the concern or are considering some step which would identify their interests with those of the business in question. The economists' search for economic facts is quite impersonal; the caution of the proprietor which may tend to an under-statement of his position may appear to the economists to be nothing more than an obstacle hiding the facts for which they are seeking. Trade creditors, bankers, and financiers would not ask for the publication of information which might be detrimental to the credit of the business and, therefore, to the interests of shareholders, but this aspect of individual ownership and responsibility which has its effect on the amount of information published does not necessarily find a counterpart in the economic viewpoint. The reconciliation of these divergent points of view is not always practicable under existing conditions, and the problem would appear to be one of social philosophy rather than accountancy.

Nevertheless, it is perhaps worthy of serious consideration by our profession, which is well-equipped for the task of guiding the many diverse influences towards a common goal which would be unattainable by divided efforts inspired by different ideals.

The direction in which advance should be sought should be rather towards satisfying the need for fuller information than towards following a technical sense of form.

On the other hand, as I have already indicated, shareholders and others for their part should recognise the limitations to which balance sheets are necessarily subject. The compilation of a series of statements showing a summary of current assets and liabilities, of capital and other resources and how they have been employed ; of normal earnings and dividends over a series of years : these and other statistics compiled from published accounts may give an accurate picture of the past and present positions, but it will be recognised that they are not necessarily the sole criterion of future success.

At the same time it is desirable to point out that much valuable information which could be extracted from published accounts is frequently lost owing to the apathy of shareholders in general. When disaster comes it is often those who were too apathetic to study the accounts in times of prosperity who are loudest in their denunciations.

It will be appreciated that in the time at my disposal to-day it has been impossible to deal with every aspect of this subject, but I have endeavoured to touch upon some of the more important points, and I can only express the hope that you will find them of sufficient interest to merit your further consideration. (Applause.)

Mr. HAROLD FITCH KEMP, F.C.A. (London), in moving a vote of thanks to Sir Gilbert, said he was sure he was voicing the opinion of everyone present when he said that his address was a remarkable one, containing as it did careful reflections on the difficulties that surrounded the preparation and presentation of balance sheets, and should be widely circulated in view of the misapprehension that existed in the public mind as to what a balance sheet was, and what it purported to show. To them, as professional men, what Sir Gilbert had told them was of great interest, but it was also of great value for a wider audience. He hoped, too, that it would be studied by many outside their profession who were interested in one form or another in the balance sheets of public companies. As to the paper, there were many points of outstanding interest, and therefore he selected for a few observations the subject of secret reserves. The subject was not free from difficulty and controversy—he believed among highly qualified professional men there was a divergence of view as, indeed, was to be expected unless and until some authoritative legal decision on the question was available for their guidance. There were decisions which gave warning against preparing a balance sheet in such a form as to give an unduly favourable view of the position if considered with reasonable care ; but so far as he knew there was no authoritative decision or any dictum of any Judge that dealt with the contrary proposition. As Sir Gilbert had said, the explanation of, and the need for, reserves was primarily a matter for directors, and their responsibility as accountants must clearly be of a secondary kind. He suggested that in deciding on the propriety of the allocation of reserves the accountant would find that his best guide was his experience, and, with it, what was called business sense ; and that that would enable him to form a better judgment as to the reasonableness of the policy proposed by directors and so, incidentally, assist the company and shareholders, who were his constituents, rather than rigid insistence on full disclosure. He did not lose sight of the fact that there was a view that there should be no secret reserves, and that all reserves should be stated on the balance sheet. He thought, however, most of them would be with him in the hope that that view would never be of general acceptance as it would tie the hands of directors, would put barriers in the way of prudent finance, and would largely destroy the efficacy of reserves, as a cushion to absorb shocks to which trade and finance must inevitably be subject.

Mr. W. B. KEEN, F.C.A. (London), seconded the vote of thanks. Such a paper as that read by Sir Gilbert could not, he said, fail to interest and instruct. The opinions expressed by him based on his wide experience and well-balanced judgment were of the utmost value. They were, therefore, much indebted to him for his paper. The author had given an extraordinarily clear and concise summary of the main points arising for consideration in dealing with a balance sheet and his discussion of the position of the auditor in relation to the sometimes conflicting interests of shareholders, directors, economists, and the public appeared to him to be specially valuable. There was, of course, a widespread demand for more information, and he thought that Sir Gilbert had said very wisely that advance should be rather towards satisfying the need for fuller information than towards following a technical sense of form. To the uninitiated a balance sheet was a very mysterious document and there could be no doubt that they should, as far as it lay with them, endeavour to make it understandable. In some instances a few words of explanation added might often make an item clear which otherwise would puzzle and mislead a simple shareholder. That was to say, if a profit and loss balance appeared among the assets it would sometimes be kind to indicate that it did not represent a profit. There were many other cases where an item which was not clear could be made clear if the auditors suggested slight modifications or an addition to the words set out on the balance sheet. The question discussed by Sir Gilbert in connection with subsidiary companies, secret reserves, fixed, as distinct from floating assets, well illustrated the difficulties and responsibilities attaching to the duties of an auditor and the impossibility of accurately defining the measure of that responsibility. They would all be glad to have an auditor's duties accurately defined and a definite limit set to his liability, but Sir Gilbert's paper must, he thought, make it clear that that was not practical politics and that the honest and careful exercise of judgment and discretion must be the auditor's protection. On the subject of depreciation and reserves, Sir Gilbert was particularly guarded when dealing with the thorny question of secret reserves. He said, and he thought they would all agree with him, that it was unwise to be dogmatic on the question, and that each case must be dealt with on its merits. An auditor was naturally glad to see liberal provision made under those headings but it was sometimes necessary to see that extravagant provision was not made, as for instance in the case of a statutory gas or water company, where the dividend to the shareholders was limited and the consumers were entitled to any remaining profit applied in reduction of charges. That was a typical case of the conflict of interests of shareholders and the public. He found it impossible to criticise the paper ; he was, in fact, full of admiration for its construction and its substance.

Mr. R. F. W. Fincham, F.C.A. (London), said that Sir Gilbert Garnsey was to be commended on his ingenuity in dealing with an old subject, i.e. the Balance Sheet, from a new angle, and he could not recollect, going back a number of years, any treatise dealing with the limitation of that document. That a balance sheet had only a limited application would, he thought, be seen clearly when one looked back to its original inception when it was merely a collection of Ledger balances, debit and credit (after the books had been closed off) and nothing more. There could be no doubt that with the progress of time and the progress of business and joint-stock activity the position had developed and that the balance sheet to-day had become a fuller document than it was : indeed, the position now was that as a rule the balance sheet was settled first and the books were made to coincide with it. Even so, it was well to recognise that a balance sheet still had many limitations. It was commonly supposed that a balance sheet showed the actual financial position, but in point of fact it was only, say, one in a hundred which did so, and this arose in part from some such circumstances as those set out by Sir Gilbert. First as to assets. In the case of land and buildings these would generally appear in the balance sheet at their original cost (which may have been 30 or 40 years ago) and had no relation to present-day values. Take the case of stock, it might be introduced at cost or market price in the ordinary way, but the value might have undergone considerable change before the balance sheet made its appearance. Take the case of trade-marks and patents ; they might appear at high value when they had little value, or might appear at little value or no value when they had great value. The same remark applied to goodwill. Then losses on Capital Account might be ignored and still be included amongst the assets. On the other hand there might be considerable appreciation in value which was not taken into account. Then as to liabilities. The average balance sheet took no account of a number of important running liabilities such as leases, service agreements and contracts entered into for future delivery. On the other hand the liabilities might include substantial sums, which, being in the nature of secret reserves, had no existence in fact. The whole point was, as Sir Gilbert had stated, that a balance sheet does not take into account the realisation factor which is often vastly different from the going concern position. The question was, what is the alternative to this admittedly incomplete state of affairs and whether there is any point in making a change. The present system had for the most part stood the test of time and was fairly well understood by people in the habit of scrutinising balance sheets. Professional accountants were aware of the limitations but what was wanted was to bring that knowledge home to the public, so that the public would not expect too much of the document and would not be surprised when reconstruction or liquidation supervened at some later date. With these observations he wished to congratulate Sir Gilbert Garnsey on his able, interesting, and timely paper, which would make a welcome addition to the literature of the profession. (Applause.)

Mr. W. CASH, F.C.A. (London), said he desired to emphasise one or two points which Sir Gilbert had raised, and heartily to join in the remarks that had been made in the attempt to estimate the value of the paper. It had brought into concise form and crystallised what he believed would be the view of those who were best qualified to speak as to what a balance sheet should contain and what the real constitution of a balance sheet might be said to be. Mr. Keen had drawn attention to the statement by Sir Gilbert that "the alterations in the law were all in the direction of affording more information," and he had pointed out that many balance sheets already gave those particulars, although the new legislation, when in force, would have the effect of standardising the best practice. He had referred to that paragraph for this reason, that it devolved upon him to consider the various amendments to the recent Bill that were put forward. He believed Sir Gilbert would agree that the Act of Parliament had made a distinct advance as to what should appear in a balance sheet, and had gone far enough as to disclosure from the point of view of shareholders, creditors and others. The author of the paper had, however, made it perfectly clear that when the new Companies Act came into operation every public company must show in the balance sheet such particulars as would disclose the general nature of the assets and the liabilities. Some members present might not know, however, the amount of pressure that was put on the Government and the Board of Trade when the Bill was in progress in the House of Commons to enforce two things—more disclosure, and the setting up of a standardised form of accounts to be applied to all balance sheets. Two things were behind that. He did not think some of those who pressed for the amendments really knew what they wanted ; it seemed to him that they simply felt a desire to press the word " disclosure " without knowing exactly what they wanted or why it should be made compulsory. They appeared to ignore the fact that what might be necessary or desirable in that relation in certain undertakings would be distinctly harmful if applied to others. There was vast variety in companies, and in the scope and character of their businesses; there were, on the one hand, manufacturing companies, and, on the other, there were banks, foreign railways, trust companies and so forth; and, therefore, to say that there should be a stereotyped form of balance sheet, involving disclosures on fixed lines, showed a lack of proper appreciation of the situation. He suggested that Parliament had gone quite far enough with regard to disclosure in asking for a setting out of the particulars which were now required. There was required the splitting up of the assets under certain heads, and making clear what were the floating assets, which were valued on a basis different from the others. He was gratified to feel that Sir Gilbert's views were in accordance with the alteration in the law which would soon come into force, and he agreed with him entirely in saying that the advance should be in the direction of more information being given rather than in a rigid adherence to a technical form in accounts. The position must vary in individual cases. He regarded Sir Gilbert's paper as a most valuable contribution to the literature of the accountancy profession.

The PRESIDENT expressed the opinion that a liberal circulation of the paper, so that it might reach the man in the street, would do much to clear up a lot of misunderstanding.

The vote of thanks was carried with acclamation.

Sir GILBERT, in reply, expressed his sense of indebtedness for the kind remarks which had been made on his paper. It had given him a certain amount of consideration and he could only hope that some of the points upon which he had touched might be of some service to members of the profession. It had been a great privilege to him to visit Birmingham where he was once one of the honorary secretaries of the Chartered Accountants Students' Society. He had experienced much pleasure in returning and he hoped he would be invited again to come to Birmingham.

At the conclusion of the afternoon session the members adjourned to the Queen's Hotel, where tea was served in the Warwick Room.

Accountancy in Transition

Edited by Richard P. Brief, NEW YORK UNIVERSITY

A GARLAND SERIES